line

Drawing · APU · Cambridge EDITED BY *Wendy Coates-Smith* AND *Martin Salisbury* No 2 **Children's books**

APU Department of
ART AND DESIGN

Hippopotamus by Květa Pacovská
taken from *One Five Many*.

line

Published by the Department of
Art and Design, Illustration Pathway.
APU, Cambridge CB1 1PT

©Text Wendy Coates-Smith,
Martin Salisbury, Jane Stanton,
Robin Harris, Nick Sharratt and
Tom Morgan-Jones 2001. Images
remain the copyright of the artists.

PRINTING
Printed in the United Kingdom
by University Printing Services,
University Press, Cambridge

PAPER
Text Fineblade Smooth 130 g/m²
Cover Hannoart Silk 350 g/m²

DESIGN
Dale Tomlinson

TYPOGRAPHY
FFQuadraat Family

ISBN 0 9537810 1 1

Cover: Květa Pacovská, letter X from *Alphabet*; on the back, Clown from *One Five Many*.
Inside front: André François, The Lost Boy's Home from *Tom & Tabby*.
Inside back: Cat from *The Art of Květa Pacovská*.

Contents

Contributors

Wendy Coates-Smith is co-editor of *Line*, Illustration part time lecturer at APU and writer on illustrators and illustration.

Martin Salisbury is co-editor of *Line*, Course Leader BA (Hons) Illustration & MA Children's Book Illustration, and a freelance illustrator.

Jane Stanton is Head of BA (Hons) Graphic Design, University of Derby, and a freelance illustrator.

Robin Harris is a freelance editorial, advertising, and book illustrator. Part time Illustration lecturer at Middlesex, Loughborough and Kingston Universities.

Nick Sharratt is a freelance editorial and book illustrator and is author/illustrator of many children's books.

Tom Morgan-Jones is a recent illustration graduate from APU and a D&AD student award winner. He works as a freelance illustrator and is a regular contributor of editorial concepts and illustrations to *Adhoc* magazine.

The editors would like to thank the artists for their time, support and the use of their work for reproduction. Special thanks to John Bodley at Faber & Faber and Richard Bawden.

4

Editorial

In *Line 2* we explore the practice of drawing in the context of the art of children's book illustration, and it's publication coincides with the launch of the new MA in Children's Book Illustration at APU. This is a unique programme and has emerged through the ongoing successes of our many students and graduates who have chosen to specialise in this area.

It is fair to say that in recent years publishing for children has experienced something of a boom, a new 'Golden Age' perhaps, during which many leading illustrators, encouraged by a recession in some other areas of publishing, have turned their hand to visual story telling for children. The picture book especially has become an important platform for the art of illustration, at a time when, with the exception of the Folio Society, we have seen a steady decline in the publication of illustrated books for adults.

In the United Kingdom we enjoy a rich heritage of artists, working in every period, who have made a significant contribution to the art of illustration for children. From the hugely popular Beatrix Potter and E. H. Shepherd, we can look back to the early chap books, and on to Blake, Bewick, Caldecott, Lear, Rackham, Tenniel, Peake and Ardizzone among the many distinguished practitioners.

A considerable amount of research has been and continues to be carried out around the subject of books and literature for children. Here we make no apologies for concerning ourselves with the subject from the perspective of the artist.

Many of the most successful picture books are 'written' and illustrated by the artist. Perhaps 'authored' is a more appropriate term. In the words of Maurice Sendak a good picture book is a 'visual poem'. This growing trend for artists to take a more authorial approach to picture books is surely a positive thing and an indication of the true nature of a vehicle for communication where a seamless relationship between word, image and design is so fundamental to its vitality.

The children's books of André François
Wendy Coates-Smith

1. *André François*, Booth-Clibborn Editions, Polygon Editions SARL, Basle, 1986.

2. *Ubu Roi*, Alfred Jarry, André François, Le Club de Meilleur Livre, Paris, 1957.

3. *The Thames and Hudson Encyclopaedia of Graphic Design and Designers*, Alan and Isabella Livingston, Thames and Hudson, London, 1992.

Clown Ploughing, an illustration commissioned for Boussac Textiles, containing a real razor blade, from Graphis 86, Nov/Dec 1959, Amstutz & Herdeg, Zurich, Switzerland.

Born in 1915 in Timisoara, Hungary, André François became a citizen of Rumania as a result of border changes after the First World War. If this silent and unwilled alteration didn't stimulate his interest in the power of magical transformation, it certainly gave rise to his suspicion of labels. While still very young he moved to Paris and adopted French nationality. This was to be the right choice in the long run, for by instinct he identified France with art, and Cassandre, the poster designer he much admired, lived and worked there. But during the Occupation, he was stripped of his adopted nationality and forced to go into hiding, with false papers, in order to survive.

Inspired to construct a world which matched his inner vision, he has quietly determined such personal history and identity he thought necessary, through his creative work. As with many other artists his vision has been formed through absorption in the world around him, and he speaks of the powerful childhood experiences which shaped his imagination:

My father had twelve brothers and two sisters. One uncle, who I never met, captured my imagination. His name was Armand, he was over two metres in height and he had run off with the circus when he was fourteen. Later on in life, he worked, amongst other things, as a sword eater and juggler, then married the widow of Salomonski, one of the great Russian circus family, and so became owner of the circuses of Moscow and Riga, as well as several travelling circuses. Stories were told of him whenever the circus came to town and I often dreamt about him.

The winters were freezing. Stalagmites sprang up when someone spat on the pavements. My sister and I spent most of our summers on a farm belonging to one of my uncles, with cows and horses. Flat wheat fields, like those of the Beauce, stretched to the horizon and I would sit and watch objects expand from tiny dots to identifiable vehicles or people as they came across the plains. Timisoara itself was a fair-sized town, with fortifications dating back to the Turkish occupation, two cinemas and trams identified by colour, rather than a route number or destination, since many people could not read. The trams ran down our street and, lying awake in bed at night, I would watch the beam from their lights track up the wall, across the ceiling and back down the opposite wall to the floor. Close to home was the town's open-air cinema and in summer I would sit on the balcony running along the front of the house to watch the silent movements of the figures on the screen. It was impossible to work out exactly what was happening, but the shadowy dramas thrilled me.[1]

Refusing to recognize values skewed to conventional hierarchies, or accepting that these have any claim on him, he has been able to defend his personal universe, or as he would say 'the world shaped to his convenience'. His love of gentle, innocent beauty – whether found in nature or the products of man – contrasts with a ferocious ability to mock and ridicule the enemy of those things.

In a typically memorable image he shows a clown ploughing a field with a razor blade. This illustration might have been produced in a sketch book, but it was designed to promote Boussac Textiles. The blade, a real blade stuck on the drawing, represents precision, yet the soil looks heavy. It would be a literal impossibility, even if the blade were enormous. The horse is beautiful, solid, and monumental, a real farm animal such as those on his uncle's farm. Guiding the blade is a clown, also muscular and with a sinister smile. Above the clown and the horse is a crescent moon, hanging between the clown and horse like a scimitar, menacingly close. Comparable in power to the dream-like images of Marc Chagall or Henri Rousseau, the poetic energy in the image is achieved with an apparent disregard for craftsmanship and it has a raw directness which is disturbing.

By way of contrast his drawings for Ubu Roi[2] deal with the exercise and abuse of power and still retain their satirical impact. In these drawings it is possible to trace the origins of a Steadman splat of ink or a Scarfe stab of the nib. So he is a propagandist as well as a poet. Deeply admired by his peers, on whom his impact is incalculable, he is not a household name here, or even on the continent where his work has been more visible. An entry for him in *The Thames and Hudson Encyclopaedia of Graphic Design and Designers*[3] states:

Allez-oop!, from *The Biting Eye.*

François has been an innovative and prolific illustrator for over five decades. Renowned for his advertising posters and covers for international journals … he has also illustrated numerous books, many for children. Increasingly working in the area of painting and sculpture, his versatility extends to designing theatre sets, having worked for a number of leading directors during the late 1950s and early 60s. Exhibitions of his work have been shown throughout the world …

The British showed an interest in his work early on. His work was commissioned for Lilliput[4] and Punch[5] and by advertising agencies such as Colman Prentice and Varley. François' innovative use of traditional materials, combined with a nimble imagination, enabled him to cast aside outmoded approaches, notably in working for advertising. His use of a scratchy line, insistent and urgent in its character, is immediately identifiable as his own, as is the signature with which he signs his work. By refusing to acknowledge constraints he sees as incompatible with a joyous interpretation of the brief, he challenged the practices of his time and created a greater freedom for himself and others. This legacy has been effortlessly passed on through the example of his own practice and only his peers and the immediately succeeding generation are aware of the huge debt owed to him. Flattered by this obvious tribute, he is nevertheless irritated by 'copying'. The influence of a powerful innovator may be necessarily diluted when filtered through the creative work of others, but it is a striking fact that his admirers, many of whom are themselves fine graphic artists, become more truly themselves for having studied his work.

That his influence may be seen in the work of many other artists is due to the liberating effects of his wit and humanity as much as the impact of his vigorous and uncompromising line. In an age when delicacy or elegance was still sought after in the advertising image, François administered the sardonic corrective of his split-nib spluttering line. In his introduction to *The Biting Eye*[6] Ronald Searle writes:

Somewhere or other, a French art critic has referred to the art of André François as a 'Trojan Horse'. The metaphor is not as obscure as it might at first seem, for the deceptively naive images that are carved by his pen have, at first glance, the touch of the child about them.

It might be argued that François deliberately places himself at a disadvantage by eschewing the sensitive line in favour of the harsh scratch; that he brushes aside popular sympathy by erecting round his work a barrier of barbs. But this crude line conceals a delicate lance which can be either

lethal or deflating … I remember a time in François' search for that 'rough' line when he systematically robbed every post office pen, over a wide area of Paris, of its traditionally unusable nib. Some of us may prefer to bandage our second fingers occasionally, as an obstacle against allowing our pens to slide into an easy line. François went to the point of contact and forced poetry out of the grandfather of nibs …

It is worth recording that even quite recently an editor refused to publish the work of François, on the ground that his sixteen-year-old daughter could do better … the academic strength and sure structure beneath the carefully-planned simplicity of François' work is in the nature of a revelation. With the advantages of an adult mind he peers through the eyes of a child and in the simplest terms restates the adventure, poetry and meanness of the world around us.

Through the power of his line he is able to present these discoveries as a statement of fact – even when the final result is sheer fantasy. In François' work the dividing line between fantasy and reality is barely visible. Ideas sprout like flowers from his head. But they are rooted in reality, not dottiness, and although the order of things is rearranged, it is only to sharpen our appreciation of them.

Driving one night with François through the darkness of a country road, the beam of his headlamps picked out two lovers walking arm in arm. As we approached them he flicked off his lights. "Did you see?" he said, "I made them disappear." … As with his dip-switch so with his pen …

Tributes from a distinguished group of artists, illustrators, and cartoonists, were reproduced on the jacket of *André François:*

'A beautiful volume dedicated to the exquisite wit and artistry of André François, one of this century's most original illustrators …' MAURICE SENDAK

'For me, as surely for other illustrators starting their professional life in the fifties, André François was the most inspiring illustrator of the time. Amongst so much cliche and convention, he seized a freedom that we all envied.' QUENTIN BLAKE

'André François, was one of my greatest influences – the first cartoonist to make me realise how much life there could be in a line.' RALPH STEADMAN

'André François is an absolute original. He was the first artist to open my eyes to the possibilities of witty and expressive drawing outside the usual conventions.' GERALD SCARFE

Many Americans could be added to that list, not least of which are Milton Glaser and Seymour Chwast of Pushpin Studios.[7] Many years ago it was a passing remark from Seymour Chwast which drew my attention to André François' books for children. Tomi Ungerer is also an

4. Lilliput, a satirical pocket magazine published monthly by Hulton in the 40s and 50s.

5. Punch, a humorous weekly news journal noted for its cartoons and caricatures began publication in the nineteenth century, no longer, despite attempts to revive it, being published.

6. The Biting Eye, a collection on work by François published by Ronald Searle and Kaye Webb, Perpetua Books, London, 1960.

7. Pushpin Studios, formed in New York in 1954 by Glaser and Chwast together with illustrators Reynolds Ruffins and Edward Sorel. Eclectic in approach the studio pioneered a new kind of stylish decorative graphics which contrasted with the prevailing influence of International Modernism.

8. *No Kiss For Mother*, Tomi Ungerer, Methuen Children's Books Ltd, London, 1974.

9. *Grodge-cat and the Window Cleaner*, John Symonds, André François, Pantheon Books, New York, 1965.

10. *Tom & Tabby*, John Symonds, Robert Delpire, André François, Paris, 1963.

11. *André François' Double Bedside Book*, Andre Deutsch, London, 1952.

artist for whom François was to be a formative influence, and his book *No Kiss for Mother*[8] is a younger cousin to *Grodge-cat and The Window Cleaner*[9] and *Tom & Tabby*[10]

But who inspired and influenced André François? Nicholas Bentley attempted to answer that question in his Introduction to André François' *Double Bedside Book*:[11]

...*The appearance of François' work in England was delayed by the war, though in the summer of 1939 the Southern Railway, with a sense of taste and enterprise painfully lacking in its successor, commissioned him to design a poster. Unfortunately, this never appeared; but it would have been interesting to see it, if only because François, after leaving the Ecole des Beaux Arts in Paris, studied first at the school, and later in the studio of A. M. Cassandre, an artist who ranks in importance with Lautrec and the Beggarstaffs in the development of poster design.*

Of Cassandre's influence little remains to be seen in François' work, though indirectly, as he says, it is still of profound importance to him... Now and then it seems possible to observe a long-distance likeness to a Thurber woman or a Thurber dog; sometimes there seems to be a touch of Steinberg, sometimes of Grosz or Picasso, another artist to whom François admits a considerable debt. Occasionally, as in a deliberate yet improbable association of certain images, there is a hint of Salvador Dali. But it is no more than a hint, for François, who is, incidentally, a man of the most engaging modesty, feels no need, and still less itch, to advertise himself or his drawings by calculated eccentricity and personal flamboyance.

Other critics and artists have tried to pin down these unique characteristics with limited success, but it is hard to improve on Bentley's explanation for his failure to find the answer:

No doubt if one were to apply the methods of Bergson or Freud or Eastman, it would be possible to get somewhere near the roots of François' sense of humour; though whether this would increase enjoyment of his work depends on how gravely you approach the subject of laughter. His preoccupation with certain recurrent and apparently unrelated themes, knight-errantry, for instance, or the tattooist's art, or the life of the cloister, may have some gloomy or involved meaning for the psychiatrist, but not for me. I cannot imagine for what reason I should want to do so, but assuming that it were necessary to try to separate the mental process from the visual, I should be stumped. François' ideas, and the highly individual technique he has evolved for their expression, seem to me as much a part of each other as his tattooed ladies are part of the gentlemen who display them.

But the emphasis here is meant to be on his books for children. Why devote space to the broader examination of his work? One reason, perhaps, is because he has successfully applied his talents to a wide range of challenges. In glancing at this wider context the originality of his achievements as an artist for children's literature becomes clearer. A study of François' work reveals that his techniques and his ideas are seamlessly applied to whatever he does, and

Illustration from *Ubu Roi*, Ubu mounts his Financial Horse.

there are no detectable areas where the work is less satisfactory or indeed where the language changes because of its origin or purpose. This is an exceptionally difficult task to achieve, and may partly explain his unique standing in the eyes of other cartoonists, illustrators and designers.

He can convincingly depict the world through the eyes of others, whether of a child or another creature. This is especially true of his work for children, where human and animal occupy the same fantastical universe as equals. He makes no distinctions of importance and is therefore not hostage to the cramping limitations of habit. All of his capacities are brought together in the most natural and unforced way when he begins to work on a text. It makes no difference to François whether the text is for adults such as Ubu Roi[12] by Alfred Jarry, or a text for children such as The Magic Currant Bun.[13]

Claude Roy wrote on François for Graphis:[14]
A perusal of his drawings and paintings leaves no doubt that the style he has created is thoroughly calculated, carefully thought out and artfully cultivated. This is not to deny that his art is basically intuitive: he would indeed protest the suggestion that he had intentionally created a style. But herein enters intelligence, critical sense. And André François here is almost faultless.

André François is an artist of the greatest dexterity. It is with deliberate intent that he has perfected, by dint of study and hard work, a technique of drawing and colouring that strikes us first of all by its wily awkwardness. He is in fact adroitly awkward, as are, in modern art, …(I am thinking of Paul Klee, Chagall and a number of others). The difficulty here is that of recovering the freshness and the dazzling awkwardness of childhood without falling foul of shallow imitation… André François has survived these dangers and has found… the candour of childhood, the freshness of vision of the ten-year old, without renouncing the discoveries and skills of maturity… I am not surprised, that in Europe, the English should have been so quick to adopt François. They recognise in him a cousin of Lewis Carroll and Edward Lear, both masters of nonsense and an unusual brand of humour.

François was very demanding about the texts he chose. One of his first books for children, Little Boy Brown,[15] was by an American author, Isobel Harris, and it was also her first book. Though François was pleased with the book, the chance to work with Harris did not come again. When Claude Roy wrote about François finding the freshness and candour of childhood without renouncing his skills of maturity he may have had in mind the books for children that François had published between 1949 and 1958, two of which were

Three illustrations from *Little Boy Brown*: **City Life, Thinking of other places and Meal with Hilda's family.**

12. *Ubu Roi*, Alfred Jarry, André François, Le Club du Meilleur Livre, Paris, 1957.

13. *The Magic Currant Bun*, John Symonds, André François, Faber and Faber, London, 1953.

14. *Graphis 76*, Amstutz & Herdeg, Zürich, 1958.

15. *Little Boy Brown*, Isobel Harris and André François, J. B. Lippincott Co., Philadelphia and New York, 1949.

of great quality, *Lettre des Iles Baladar*[16] by Jacques Prévert and *The Magic Currant Bun* by John Symonds.

If for some reason the partnership with Harris and Prévert did not lead to other books, the relationship with John Symonds was to flower. They had first met when Symonds worked at Lilliput, and a mutually beneficial working relationship developed from their friendship. As both men had a powerful attraction to fantasy and the whimsical, each fed the imagination of the other. Symonds had written five novels before the fifth was published in 1947 by Samson Low, with illustrations by François. Of their young author, Samson Low wrote 'We decided to publish this unusual novel because we believe that the author has a genuine imaginative gift, and that behind his imagery and caricature there is a deep human experience and sympathy'.[17] The same might equally be said of François. François' drawings were typical of those he had been doing for Lilliput, and not indicative of the work he later produced for *Lettre des Iles Baladar*. Of the thirteen books Symonds wrote for children, six were illustrated by François, with others by Edward Ardizzone,[18] James Boswell,[19] Gerard Hoffnung,[20] Pauline Baynes[21] and Pamela Bianco.[22]

Symonds also wrote thirteen novels for adults, and several plays for stage, radio and television.

16. *Lettre des Iles Baladar*, Jacques Prévert and André François, Le Point du Jour, Gallimard, Paris, 1952.

17. Jacket flap for *William Waste*, John Symonds, André François, Samson Low, London, 1947.

18. *Lottie*, Edward Ardizzone, Lane, 1957; *Elfrieda and The Pig*, John Symonds, Edward Ardizzone, Harrap, London, 1957; and *The Stuffed Dog*, John Symonds, Edward Ardizzone, Dent, London, 1967.

19. *Dapple Grey, The Story of a Rocking Horse*, John Symonds, James Boswell, Watts, New York, 1962.

20. *The Isle of Cats*, John Symonds, Gerard Hoffnung, Laurie, London 1955, revised edition Scholar Press, London, 1979.

21. *Harrold: The Story of a Friendship*, John Symonds, Pauline Baynes, Dent, London, 1973.

22. *Away to the Moon*, John Symonds, Pamela Bianco, Lippincott, Philadelphia and New York, 1956.

23. *Twentieth-Century Children's Writers*, ed. D. L. Kirkpatrick 2nd edition, Macmillan Publishers, 1983.

24. *Jacques le Fataliste*, Denis Diderot, André François, Les Editeurs Francais Reunis, Paris, 1946.

Twentieth-Century Children's Writers[23] has an entry for Symonds written by Margaret Campbell:

John Symonds' fantasies are shorter than most novels for older children, and his stories move quickly: they can be enjoyed by anyone over the age of about seven. Toys speak, and have problems; children or playthings from the past meet children from this century and create a mutual understanding…

She might have added that human and animal characters have shared adventures in which their emotions and perils are experienced in a way which is consistent with their character rather than their species. *Cats* in particular stirred Symonds' imagination, and three of the thirteen books for children had cats in leading roles.

Of the books written by Symonds with illustrations by François, three are featured here: *The Magic Currant Bun*, *Tom & Tabby* and *Grodge-cat and the Window Cleaner*. But these were not his first published books, and show him as a mature and assured artist, paradoxically moving from one style to another, using now one medium and now another. With François this is not a sign of confusion or uncertainty, as it might be with others. Rather it is a feature of the artist whose identity is not linked to a process or methodology but a sign of an artist moving through creative experiments at a profound level of invention, immersed in bringing another's partly realised vision fully into being.

Part of what Quentin Blake called 'a freedom that we all envied' was the hall mark of François' insouciant daring. The break between *William Waste* 1947 and *Little Boy Brown* in 1949, shows him leaving the decorative, ironic flourishes behind. He states in *André François*:

Although I wanted to find a style that was more than a convention, the stylistic simplification really came through the course of work, just as handwriting defines itself through the practice of writing. When I illustrated Jacques le Fataliste[24] by Diderot, for Aragon, for instance, the year after the war ended, I used a rather complicated and baroque style which ran against everything else being done at that time. A few years later my first children's book was published in America – Little Boy Brown – and in 1952, having met Jacques Prévert, I did the illustrations for Letter des Iles Baladar… He encouraged my unconventional approach and the book freed me from most of my mannerisms.

The story of *Little Boy Brown* concerns a comfortable, well-brought-up child, whose life has become stifling. Through a visit to the countryside with their maid Hilda, he meets her relations and makes new friends, including their dog. The freedom of their lives, compared with the constraints of the city, introduces him to an awareness of other possibilities and he learns to feel less lonely through his memories of the happy day. Though François had not himself visited America at this stage, he describes a big American city in convincing terms and shows the visible crowding and pressure, conveying the real excitement of city life. He does so in such a way that there is no negative comparison between city life and the countryside, simply an awareness of 'otherness'. He demonstrates, by means of a flattened perspective, that the tunnels are

both a limitation and a protection. He also describes the joy of the boy when the dog leans its muzzle on his lap. But perhaps the most startlingly original image describes this text:

> At twelve o'clock Hilda's father came home from his grocery shop to have his lunch. Hilda's family are smarter than we are. They can all speak two different languages, and they can close their eyes and think about two different countries. They've been on the ocean, and they've climbed mountains…

François dispenses with the cartoon bubble to signify thought, and instead, with his characters sitting side by side, shows their eyes closed and their thoughts gently moving upwards to form a communal vision of their other life. With the abandonment of conventional picture space he can make us aware of the boy's feelings about the empty bus or the crowded lift, and finally the happy dreaming in his house, where he can make the dog, the cake and a bird co-exist with the hotel corridors and the lift.

All these are reconciled in a sweetly warm illustration which is not in any way sentimentalised.

Lettre des Iles Baladar is both an entertaining story for children, about how the security and happiness of an island people is threatened from without, and an allegory of the Occupation. The people and the setting are exotic. The inhabitants of the islands are happy, careless and take their peace for granted. With the arrival of the invaders and the introduction of slave labour the false confidence of the islanders is exposed, leaving them unprepared and defenceless. The objective is the gold which the invaders discover, not simply territorial expansion. Flattered by an official appointment and a uniform, the central character, the formerly happy-go-lucky road sweeper, is almost persuaded to betray his friends. He has a vision of his fall in a nightmare where he is mocked by his neighbours. This has the effect of causing him to repent. Eventually the overweening pride and greed of the invaders brings about their downfall – and the recovery of peace by the islanders of Baladar.

François sees that the complex ambiguities of the story are given appropriate emphasis by the clever use of symbol. The grandiosity of the officials who have come to manage the islands is expressed in elaborate uniforms, regalia and statuary. Prévert invented a General who wears a peaked cap with two peaks, so that even in in retreat he is not thought to be running away. For the nightmare of the hero, François adopts creatures such as occur in the fantasies of Hieronymous Bosch. Fish with legs, a laughing man in the moon, hideous creatures underline the monkey's shame. There he is in his braided uniform and sword – a figure of fun. The magic of the moving pictures becomes the final symbol of the islander's dreams. Drawing on his childhood remembrance of the outdoor cinema, François shows the characters marching in procession, free of the screen, into the sky, happy ever after. Prévert puts it something like this:

> Because the people of the Great Continent had on their departure also abandoned a talking picture show, somehow

Three illustrations from *The Magic Currant Bun*: **The bun speaks, Raising the alarm, The chase.**

eaten one at a time will grant a wish. The story is quite wonderfully absurd, and might have amused, but also baffled, a lesser illustrator. For the theft of the bun the boy is taken to the Bastille where a rat grabs some of the bun and finds, like the boy, that eating a currant allows him to have his wish granted. The rat becomes a jailer. François shows us how the rat grows, and gains a jailer's uniform in one image by overlapping one drawing on another.

With his second wish, the rat transforms the prison into a Swiss cheese. The pace is fast and everyone is constantly taken by surprise. How to illustrate this without literally repeating the text in pictures? And could these hope to rival the narrative in excitement? There is a full page illustration on every alternate page, opposite the text. This formula, common also to his earlier books, is a real page-turner, and François never falters, running with the field, stopping only to dip his pen from time to time. The twenty full page green and black drawings contain enough energy and surprises to make the magic work. The illustrations show the action in long shots, aerial views and close-ups and he book has the pace of a silent movie chase. If the inspiration for *The Magic Currant Bun* owes something to the cinema, the two books by Symonds which followed are profoundly literary.

Apart from his love of cats, Symonds has a great admiration for the Victorian novelists. Their influence informs the atmosphere and texture of both *Tom & Tabby* and *Grodge-Cat and the Window Cleaner*. Symonds was born in 1914, and according to the jacket information for *William Waste*, had an unconventional education:

> At the age of 16 he obtained with difficulty a ticket to the Reading Room of The British Museum – the so-called 'poor man's university' – and began, as he says himself, 'when hardly literate and under the age when one is permitted to use the place,' to educate himself at his leisure and to his fancy… He believes that he has discovered, through the experience of writing…, the imaginative world to which he belongs.

If *Grodge-cat and the Window Cleaner* has a whiff of Wilkie Collins, then certainly *Tom & Tabby* has all the loved characteristics of Charles Dickens. But this is Dickens crossed with Lewis Caroll. The 'cinematic' qualities of the chase in *The Magic Currant Bun*, are missing in these two books. Here the characters are closely related to each other, and their destinies are interconnected. The atmosphere is noticeably more serious, especially in *Tom & Tabby*. Not all the characters find a happy ending, and one fears for the governess in *Grodge-cat*. She could be a character in Wilkie Collins, spotted from time to time in the crowd, with her tray of matches, her evenings lonely and her future uncertain.

Tom & Tabby begins with a young boy visiting his cat school caretaker for tea, and the cottage bursting into flames. The incongruity of a cat caretaker is discussed, but only in order to introduce other fantastical elements, and the surreal atmosphere is rapidly established as the basis for the story. As the boy is in trouble with the School Attendance Officer, and the cat has burned his

the natives got it to work just to find out what was inside. In short, newsreels, military parades, documentaries about peacock hunting. Then they made cinema themselves, like they make bread. And on the big white screen, as high as a cliff, they saw pass by, lit by the moon, everything that came to their minds, all that came from their hearts…

A year after the publication of this book François started work on *The Magic Currant Bun*. The liberating effects of working with Prévert combined with his innovations for *Little Boy Brown* provided the ideal foundation for the adventure with *The Magic Currant Bun*. As with the other books this was a two colour project. After brown and black and yellow and black it was now green and black. In each case the second colour is a tint, combined with black half-tone. François knows exactly how to use his second colour. Sometimes decoratively, other times in an ironic, witty way.

This story is a gift, a chase with magical events which are granted by the bun. Situated in Paris, François has his pick of places to draw, starting with the Eiffel Tower, Les Invalides, The Bastille, the Champs Elysee and the Arc de Triomph.

The hero gets into trouble because he tries to respond to a cry for help from a currant bun. For the bun is going stale in the bakery and wants to be rescued. The bun takes responsibility for guiding the boy away from the bakery owner, his wife, daughter, a dog, a fat lady in a hat and twenty seven and a half policemen, and the chase is on. The half policeman is small and will not only become full size, but bigger, by the end of the story. The bun explains that the currants,

own cottage down by accident, the cat and the boy decide to run away together. After a short skirmish with a ticket collector, they board a train for London where Tabby's friend Simon lives, and runs a toy shop.

On the train Tom and Tabby meet a fat boy dressed in velvet, and the giggling sisters. When the fat boy throws Tabby's pipe from the window, Tabby responds by knocking his straw hat off. While looking for the lost cat's home, Tom is propelled into the lost boy's home, but Tabby is rejected. When Tom is ushered into the vast dormitory for lost boys, a furry face peeps out from the one empty bed – it is of course Tabby.

The School Attendance Officer reappears like a pantomime villain. But the friends find a taxi cab to take them to The Toy Shop in Threadneedle Street. An unpleasant boy in a bowler hat refuses to explain where Simon is. Tom and Tabby find the back entrance to the shop, where the broken dolls are waiting for treatment. In the process of trying to mend a one-legged doll, they are discovered by the School Attendance Officer, and escape with the doll Lottie, now supported by a doll's crutch, and set off for a Sugar Mouse Shop in St Paul's Churchyard. Reunited, Simon and Tabby decide that they should go to a party being held by Lord Cherrymantle at Berkley Square in honour of his daughter. Lottie goes with them in the carriage. When they arrive they find the velvet boy is waiting to sing. The bowler-hatted boy is a spy for the School Attendance Officer, and betrays the friends to him.

But Lord Cherrymantle shuts the door on the School Attendance Officer. Tabby plays the piano. The party becomes a cake and jelly battle, attracting the attention of poor boys and girls in the streets. The velvet boy has been eating all this while, and now cannot get through the door. Tabby saves the day by giving him a contemptuous look which shrivels him, and so he runs away. Burdened by the back-log of unrepaired dolls,

Simon gives his other business, the Sugar Mouse shop, to his friend Tabby. The two friends are no longer lost, and the threat of the School Attendance Officer has dissolved

As with Dickens, coincidence plays a large part – in fact the story is driven by coincidence. The principal characters survive the terror of pursuit by the School Attendance Officer, the broken dolls find happiness through repair, the velvet boy is silenced and Tom and Tabby enjoy a shared life with an assortment of sugar mice.

François demonstrates a masterly control of mood. He lays washes of sepia and applies thick layers of

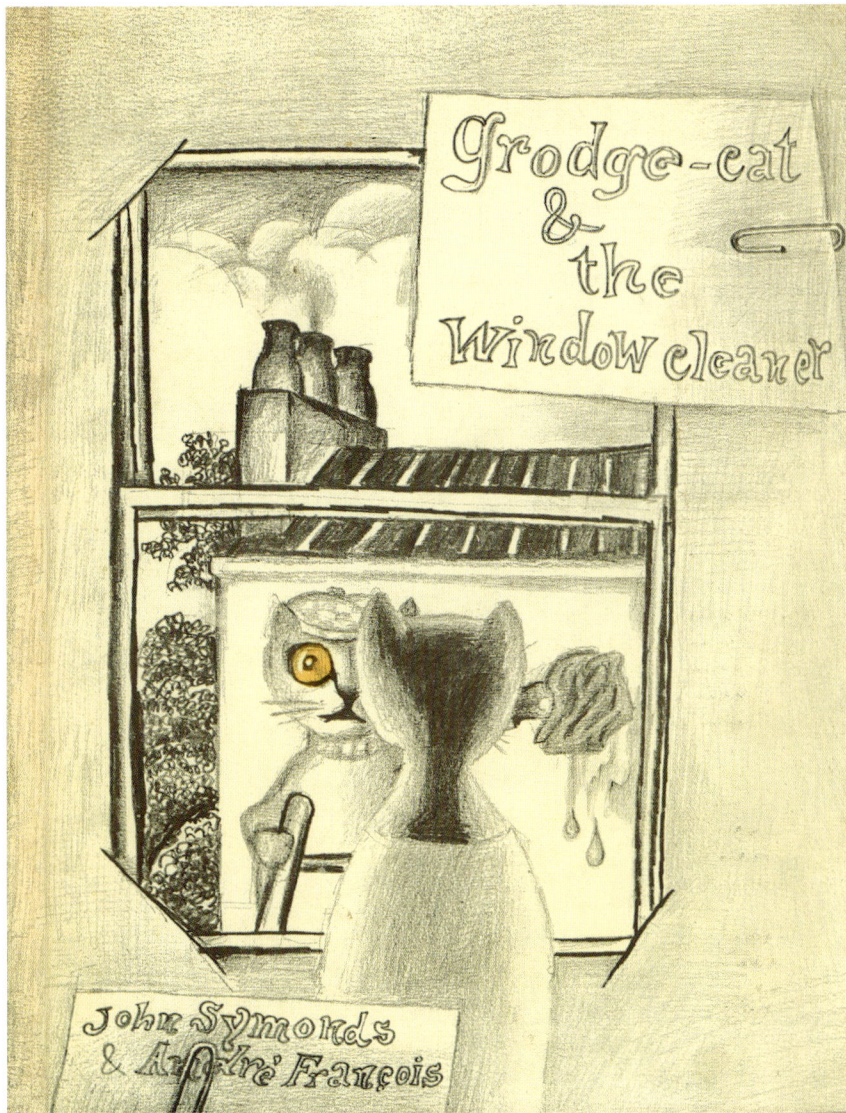

paint. While still wet, some areas of thick paint are removed to reveal the paler sepia washes underneath. The effect suggests the patina of events and the weight of passing time. The compositions are dramatic and powerful, often with a feeling of menace. Buildings are large and dark against the skyline, making the human and animal figures seem more exposed to their fate. This is especially true of the inside of the railway station, the murky dark of the Toy Shop interior or Tom and Tabby peering between the railings of the Lost Boys Home.

By comparison Grodge-cat has a sunlit quality of a summer afternoon in a congenial part of middle-class suburbia. That does not mean however that there is no lurking danger. It is illustrated in lead pencil and washes of yellow watercolour. François grasps the peculiarly English nuances and presents the characters in a series of pencil drawn images as they might appear in a Victorian photograph album. An idiosyncrasy is the use of the front pages as the album itself, so that all the illustrations appear in the first fifteen pages, including the title page, not counting the use of a double spread to show the painting, Conversation Piece.

The essential contradiction of rendering the 'photographic' images with pencil is quite deliberate and part of the joke. The pencil study of the governess caught in a blurry photograph taken from the window of a moving bus underlines the poignant vulnerability of Miss Woods and her social position. But it also tells us that it is only a story because the central device of pencil rendered 'photographs' is an absurdity in itself.

Grodge-cat and the Window Cleaner is a love story, and in the tradition of thwarted romantic love. Symonds places

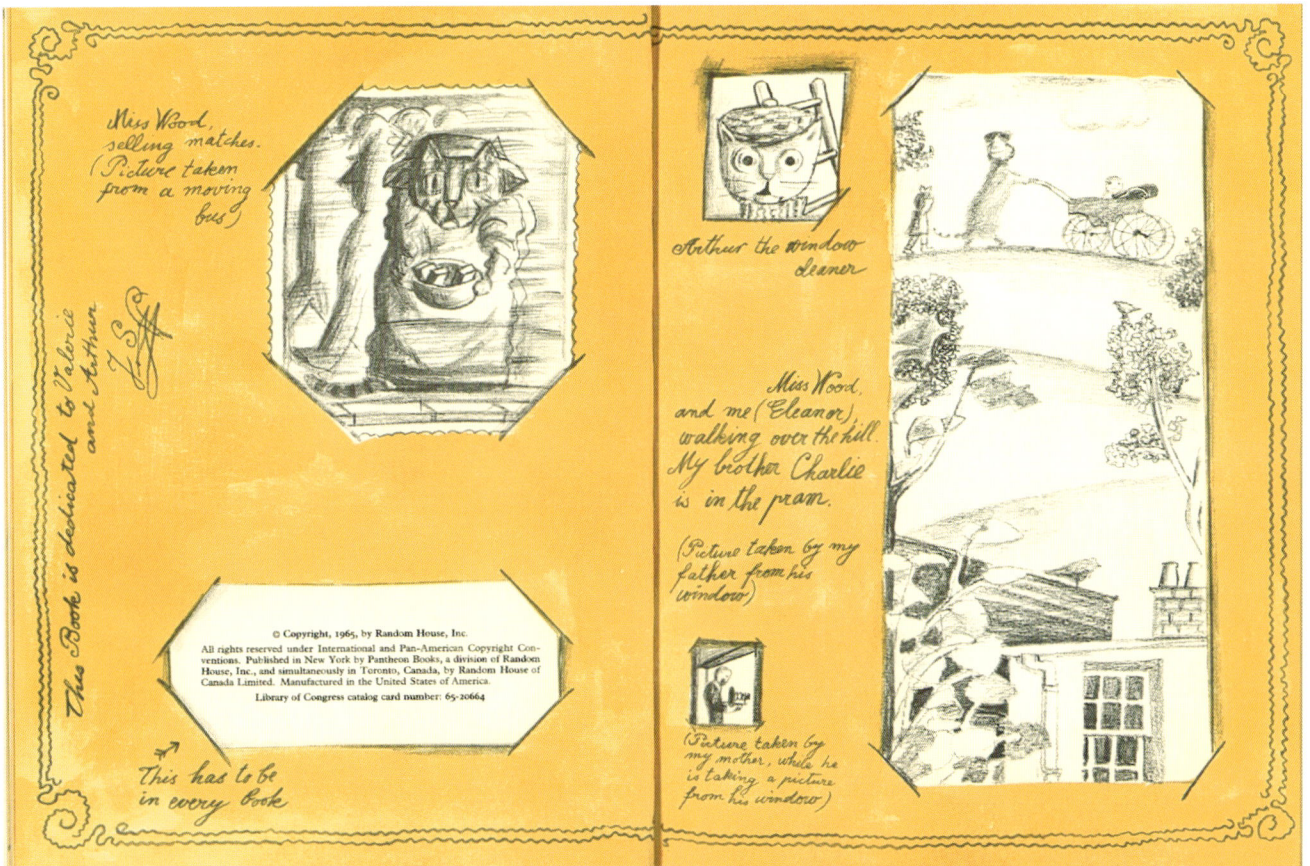

Cover and inside spread from *Grodge-cat and the Window Cleaner*. The inside spread shows the characters in the story in 'photographs' taken for the album. Miss Woods is blurred because the image was obtained from the window of a moving bus.

—but he could not see his sister anywhere. And so he swam a little more, and then he leaped up, shouting: "Mother!"

—but his mother was nowhere to be seen. And so he swam some more, and when he came up for air he called: "Father!"

20

21

the story in the latter part of the 1880s and therefore relationships reflect English manners and the clearly defined class system of Victorian England. There are masters and servants, and for them the possibility of losing one's place and thus becoming vulnerable to chance. The introductory paragraphs tell us what to expect:

> The fun begins when Grodge, an independent tortoise-shell cat, runs away from home because her father does not approve of Arthur the window-cleaning cat, who is her beloved. Soon Arthur joins her, and then Eleonor, our little-girl narrator, runs off with Sebastian Growler, a clever mongrel dog who has a professional plate-spinning act.
>
> Well, while Grodge-cat makes marrow-bone soup at their cottage in Islington, Arthur works at his job as rat catcher in the sewers – until he meets up with the rat with the Longest Tail... Meanwhile Eleonor spends her time watching Sebastian do his plate-throwing act (top of the bill at the Palladium) until they meet up with the man in the bowler hat. There is more than one breathless chase to come. First you meet them all in Eleonor's picture album. Then, on with the story!

In John Malcolm Brinnin's Arthur the Dolphin Who Didn't See Venice[25] the narrative is a slender thread on which François' drawings are strung, the story being simply that of a child that loses sight of its parents. Arthur becomes excited by a man in a small boat, and begins a playful game chasing and making bubbles. But...as any child knows who leaves his sister, mother father

and grandfather behind in order to play with a stranger, you can get lost. Arthur is lost, and quite devastated to discover this. But he is lost in Venice, and Venice is quite wonderful to look at. François chooses a stubby black crayon and a ruddy indian red wash. Arthur is charming and sensitively drawn in contrast to the dramatic Venetian scene. Arthur's landscape before he is lost is that of the bodies of the other dolphins, but in Venice this becomes alien, claustrophobic and crowded. Eventually he is found and happy to rediscover the family he had lost. Much of the impact of the pages is created by the scale of what François draws but which Arthur barely understands. Barges and gondolas cross and criss cross the pages, closing Arthur in and making him look very small.

Scale is perhaps one of the keys to François' visual imagination. All his drawings make perfect use of the page and the compositional possibilities, but these judgements are made in the context of many other considerations such as attention to period details, architecture, clothing, furniture, everyday objects – brought together with an eye for those elements which express the absurdities of human existence, and animal too of course. The effect is to focus the mind on the struggle to make accident coherent and to make sense of chance. François establishes the line between pathos and slapstick with a gentle sensitivity which is unique.

Double spread from Arthur the Dolphin Who Didn't See Venice.

25. Arthur the Dolphin Who Didn't See Venice, John Malcolm Brinnin, André François, Little, Brown & Co. in association with Atlantic Monthly Press, Boston and Toronto, 1961.

In conversation with André François

What made you want to go to art school?

I only had one hesitation I would say, it was either to be a medical student or an art student, but I think I became an artist because I was very bad at school. I was especially bad at mathematics. I started drawing at eleven or twelve. I didn't decide, things were decided for me. Very often I made no decisions, and eventually chose between two things which proposed themselves, but I didn't make decisions.

I first saw your work in the pages of my father's copies of *Lilliput*, and later whole articles in *Graphis*. There didn't seem to be any difference between your drawings for advertising, and drawings which might have been for your own pleasure. You managed to work in the least compromised way that I have seen of any artist.

When I was in advertising people asked me to produce a poster or something and I would introduce in their problem my preoccupation of the moment. In many cases, I always, not always, but pretty soon refused to do roughs. Art directors wanted you to produce roughs and once you have produced a lot of roughs they take three or four and say 'Now put all this in one.' I said now you have asked me to solve this problem I will not produce roughs, you take it or you reject it because if it is good enough it is no longer a 'rough', or if it isn't good enough there is no point in showing it. The other thing is that if you show a rough then people try to imagine what the finished thing will be like, and its got nothing to do with what you eventually produce. There were a few commissions which I didn't get because I wouldn't do roughs.

The work is vivid and alive because you didn't compromise. Some of it was done long ago, but it doesn't seem so because it doesn't reflect the norms of the period.

Well you know that was one of my criteria. The difference between painting and photography, and illustration before that, is that photography has transformed the present into the past, and painting transforms the past into the present, and that is very essential I think. Illustration is somehow very often between the two because some illustration dates.

In *André François* you spoke of wanting to go to Paris. What did you want from Paris?

I had finished college at 16 or so and done the Baccalaureate and wanted to go to art school, but my parents said Paris was too dissipated and dangerous. There was a young boy, a little older than me, who went to university in Budapest. My home was about 200 kilometres from Budapest and it seemed pretty close. My parents said that I could share with this boy, who was studying medicine and therefore serious. 'He will take care of you!' But I was very often sitting on the landing to our room till one o'clock, two o'clock in the morning because he had a girlfriend. Finally I spent about a year and a half in the School of Beaux Arts, in Budapest, and I hated every minute of it.

When you are 17 you are very cruel. In my second year each master had two rooms, one for nude and one for portrait. I did two unforgivable things: I drew her full length, and she looked so pale and under-nourished that I bought a bottle of milk, and put that in the picture. The shape of the milk bottles in those days was very beautiful. I had very little idea about politics, but the master came in and he became hysterical about this, saying 'I won't tolerate communist propaganda!' So I left the room. From that moment I would leave whenever he came in, two or three times a week, to look at the drawings. At the end of the year you had to show your work and have an interview with your master. I told him 'Not only are you a bad master, but you are a bad painter too!' After that I went down to the Secretary to leave before they could dismiss me. Then I went to Paris.

You knew of Cassandre and liked his work, but what drew you to him?

He was very important, a designer of posters and typefaces. I had seen things about him in Budapest. After a fortnight I managed to meet him and he said 'Well, I am opening a school, and you can come to that school.' It was of course a private school and pretty expensive and what it cost to study was pretty much what I had for a living. I told him and he said 'It doesn't matter, you don't pay!' But the school didn't last long because he would throw out the people who paid, and keep the people who didn't. There was another poster artist, Paul Colin, a contemporary of Cassandre. He was very different and he had about sixty students in his private school. Those who liked Cassandre despised Colin.

Did you draw from everyday life, things in your home or in the streets?

I did sketches of friends, portraits. I pretty soon discovered that I could make a caricature portrait of people and that's about all. My parents had been comfortably off until the thirties brought economic crisis and economic collapse everywhere, and so very much later after I left Cassandre I had to make a living. Maybe the fastest, easiest way to do that was to draw for the papers because you soldiered on, you got your money and it was very successful. For many years it made me produce cartoons, which I probably would not have done if I hadn't needed to earn a living. But I think that there's nothing lost, never, because it taught me a lot of things. To produce the cartoon is a work of precision.

The Biting Eye contains a broad selection of your work, drawings on location, cartoons, advertising drawings, designs for the ballet, and a lot of wonderful ideas which belong to no particular category – but which are joyful celebrations of the crazy and the unexpected.

They were from a joyful time because life was. I don't know if it comes from the scriptures or the Bible or if it's solely in readings in French. 'Que ma joie demeure', how do you translate it into English? 'I would like that my happiness might last, stay, I wish my pleasure or my happiness stayed', and it is very beautiful, certainly it exists in English, this quotation, 'que ma joie demeure' and actually people ask, 'Why do you paint or draw?' and that has been one of my answers really.

How do you react to those comments by Searle where he remarks on the use of the metaphor 'Trojan Horse' by a critic describing your work?
I think that I'd say that very, very, few people are sensitive to art or painting general speaking. You have to cheat by producing art at the same time as answering the brief. You have to cheat. If you didn't they wouldn't accept your ideas.

In these years your output was tremendous. This suggests a compulsion to work – maybe 'work' is the wrong word. You enjoy it. In a sense it is like playing.
Yes, partly, but its also self-preservation. Everything can be traced back to your instinct for preservation, such as when you carve your name, your age and so on. You are not consciously, but unconsciously certain to mark the place. To leave a trace, that's one of the reasons. I worked all the time and I was both busy and very lazy and I didn't dare to stop working. Then it is also to create a world to my convenience.

If that world hadn't been so coherent or convincing then you would not have done the books for children in the way that you did. This was the foundation from which the books emerged.
Well the other thing is we had our children pretty early, and that probably made me start doing children's books. But I didn't make a conscious decision to do children's books. In 1939 I was waiting to be called up by the French army, but that was stopped by the French armistice. Nobody was prepared for what happened, everything was completely dislocated. So we went to a place in the South of France with Pierre, who was three weeks old. I had started work for the papers before we left Paris and that was the only way to make a living.

Maybe a few poster designs. I always remember the first poster I did for Galleries Lafayette. Cassandre sent me to them. After the German occupation it got worse and worse. Within two years it became almost impossible to work for the papers because there were two zones, the occupied zone and the free zone. We were in the free zone, but then the Germans invaded the whole place. Immediately after the war there was a sort of explosion of newspapers, and new papers published. So again there was a facility for making a living with drawings in the press because it was money straight away. But I must say that I was doing my best for the papers. I took it very seriously and I always tried to do my best.

My first recognition was in Britain. I went to England for the first time in 1947 when Margaret's parents came back to England. We went to visit them and I started to submit drawings. *Lilliput* was very good and bought drawings. I met John Symonds, who was

on the staff. I met Ronald Searle and Henry.[26] We didn't live in England. Henrion and I became friends, also Kenneth Bird (Fougasse) who bought my drawings for *Punch*.

I approached Malcolm Muggeridge, the editor of *Punch*, and asked him to commission me to go to Greece. I longed to go to Greece and we had very little money. I went to Greece and sent drawings to *Punch*. I took the *Odyssey* under my arm and I drew everything. Margaret found a caption from the *Odyssey* to fit my drawings. We stayed two and a half months and I did a lot of drawings.

Then I went to Germany with Robert Delpire. Bucheim was publishing *Les Larmes de Crocodile*.[27] For many years I had refused to speak German. It was a very strange experience when I had visited Munich. Bombs had destroyed parts of the city and people were still dressed in bits of uniform. Its a complicated thing to trace your past in Europe. My father came from a Hungarian family and on my mother's side it was Austrian, and I started speaking Hungarian first, then German and Rumanian at school. My grandmother spoke German, and so when I first went to Germany in 1951 it was like in the fairy tales – for the first time in my life I understood everything they said. It was very strange.

Your first big success with children's books was *Little Boy Brown*, which was published in America.
Yes, it was reprinted many times.

Shortly after the success of *Little Boy Brown*, you met Jacques Prévert. Tell me about that.
That was *Lettre des Iles Baladar*. It was published by a branch of Gallimard, Le Point du Jour. Anyway, they introduced me to Jacques Prévert. When I first met him he was staying in the Hotel du Beaujolais – which doesn't exist any more. All of its windows looked down on the Jardins of the Palais Royal. It was very beautiful, cheap and rather decayed in those days, and he was living there. We met and talked. He proposed that we do a book together, and I was very enthusiastic about it. I used to cycle to the station at Pontoise and travel into

26. F. H. K. Henrion, designer and art director in an advertising agency who commissioned poster designs, among other things, from François.

27. *Les Larmes de Crocodile*, André François, Collection Dix sur Dix, Robert Delpire, Paris, 1956.

Two drawings made on location for *Punch*, from *The Biting Eye*.

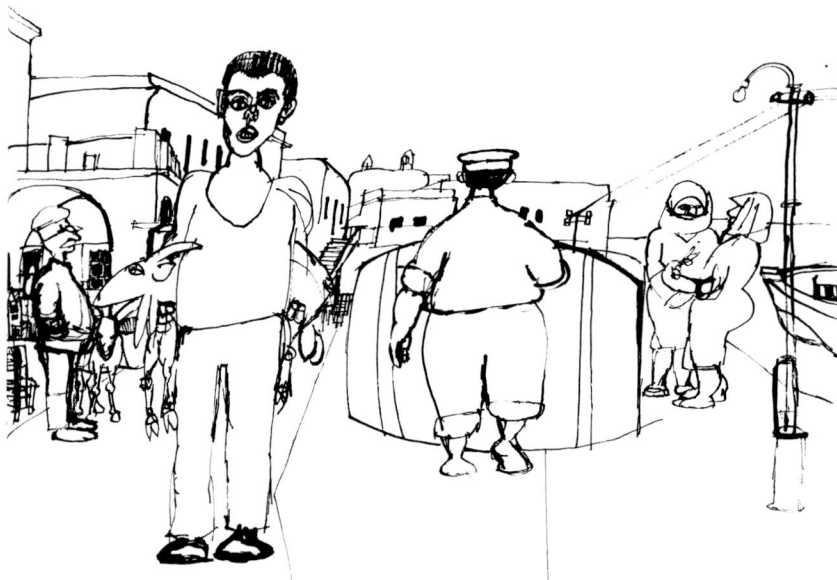

Two pages from *Les Larmes de Crocodile* also called *Crocodile Tears*, 1956, from André François.

Cartoon and cover from *The Penguin André François.*

Paris. He had a story about an island, and started telling it to me, one page at a time. It was not written down. I did the drawings and I went back and he said 'Yes, that's alright', and he would tell me a bit more. Then finally it became almost like a political pamphlet because it was an allegory of the Occupation. After seven or eight meetings I finished my drawings and he wrote the story.

In *André François* the artist tells us how his work developed generally, and something of the unique character of his commissioned work.

We were both very happy with the end product – a children's story that was, on another level, an adult allegory.

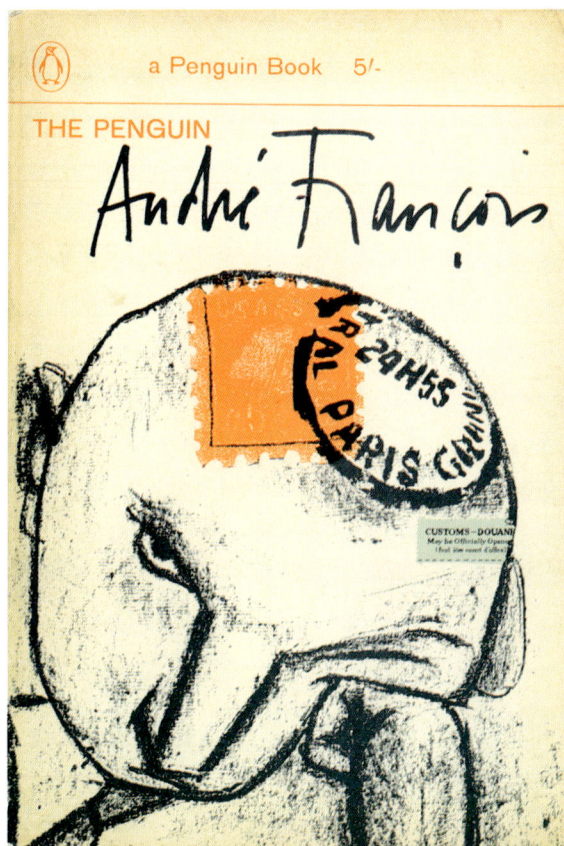

He encouraged my unconventional approach and the book freed me from most of my mannerisms.

At this time, in an initially haphazard way, I began to do more cartoons and editorial work. At a basic level, this was a way of earning a living, but it quickly became far more than that. I became caught up in the pleasure and interest of the very particular drawing language required and I was bitten by the challenge of professionalism. This was not easy at first, especially since French humour then tended to be broad rather than biting, verbal rather than visual.

The first outlets I found were the English satirical magazines, Lilliput and Punch, who were far more open to my sense of humour. Equally I can remember how amusing and appealing I found English eccentricity on my outings across the channel at this time … I loved the pubs, the docks, the beauty of the parks and river … Soon afterwards, I began to find outlets in France, too, some of them in a more political vein, working for the newspapers and magazines of the Left … In particular I began to do weekly cartoons for La Tribune des Nations … I was allowed to express my opinions quite freely, so the connection lasted a long time … Editorial work led me on to advertising and other forms of illustration in America and England as well as France…

Many other projects came through Robert Delpire … One collaboration was the children's book, Les Larmes de Crocodile, which was eventually published in seventeen countries… There were commissions outside advertising, too, and collaborations with other people…a set of playing cards for Simpson's of London, commissioned by Natasha Kroll…and I illustrated many other books. The most memorable was Alfred Jarry's extraordinary, anarchic Ubu Roi, commissioned by Massin, satirising the emptiness and stupidity of petit bourgeois values and life.

Later, in the fifties, I was asked to do my first stage design, by Roland Petit for the ballet Le velo magique and I went on to do costumes and decor for theatre including several Royal Shakespeare Company productions…

During those years I never completely gave up painting. There were periods when I would stop due to lack of time, but I would be carried back by a sudden surge of nostalgia, as if compelled by a survival instinct. In that sense the desire to paint is not an aim or ambition but an imperative means of

self-expression… Slowly I discovered the secret charm of the
countryside where we lived, the subtleties of its landscapes.
When we went to the sea I would often draw from life…

I have never completely abandoned graphics. As an
independent source of income, they have given me an enviable
freedom from commercial constraints in my painting. Besides
that I do not believe there is a clear line between working from
commission and painting, though there is one great difference.
In the first you are looking for a solution at somebody else's
instigation and in the second you are delving inside yourself.
As a result my approach to graphics has changed; I work best
with a loose rein and less fixed concept at the outset. All my
work for The New Yorker, for instance, was done within an
easy, informal arrangement that laid down no guidelines:
the art director James Geraghty's definition of a New Yorker
cover was, quite simply, a painting or drawing with The New
Yorker printed over it…

I once had a rather similar arrangement for book covers
with Penguin Books – the art editor Germano Facetti, allowed
me to choose from the list of forthcoming titles … It is more
difficult to find the same freedom within advertising concepts;
you have to create that space yourself. Over the years I have
become known for needing a free hand and, in part, due to that,
a fair number of exhibition, film and general cultural posters
have come my way.

**There are clues to his attitude to his art, and how he
achieves his effects in his last statement in** *André François.*
*Often I use fragments of reality – a pebble, a piece of driftwood,
a butterfly, even a word – as an inroad around which I can build
an image. There is a great need for such a reference point of
palpable reality, like the element of truth that makes a lie credible.
The Dutch writer, Hartog, wrote in The Lost sea of story-tellers
who went on board a ship to entertain the sailors with their tales.
The sailors enjoyed the tales and named the story-tellers the liars.
This is not an insult. But in our own age there is a great desire
for confirmation of reality: the popularity of photography is
one expression of that. By comparison, painting is a construction
of the artist, so a recognisable fragment of reality helps to create
the space for freedom of invention in the rest of the painting.
Invariably the reality then takes on its own meaning, just as
objects do in our everyday lives.*

*When I first included clock faces in collages and paintings,
for instance, I did so simply because I found them so satisfying
graphically. Then, gradually, they became meaningful: the
immobility of the circle, the passing of time, the season of
winter. Butterflies represent the passing of time for me through
their beauty: there is a dizzying sensation, a free fall through
time, in contemplating the creation of that perfection of beauty.
A butterfly has such sensuality, as well. After a while, it becomes
impossible to disentangle those multiple meanings. In the same
way, the circus embodies both my childhood excitement and the
fascination of everyday life paraded in the microcosm of the ring.*

*Those shared resonances make me think of my work as
talismans. I do not believe in art for art's sake. A painting is not
for us enacting a ritual gesture on behalf of the whole community
– as by priests in certain African tribal societies. Rather it is an
expression of a personal maladie, although hopefully others
will find in it the expression of their own feelings. The fantasy is
always inspired by a shared reality, like the echoes from a cry
across a lake. The artist simply provides a sounding board.*

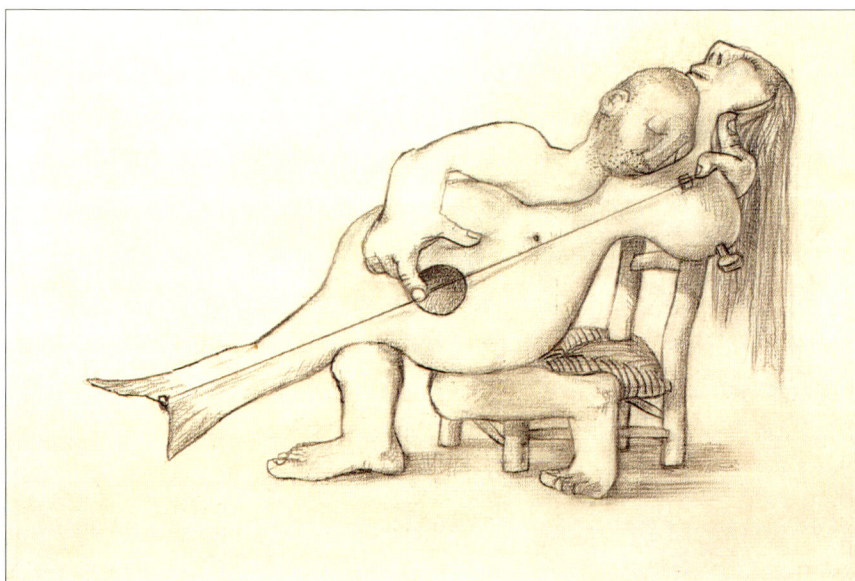

Three approaches to a favourite theme –
mermaids. The collage demonstrates François'
use of real objects which allows the interplay
between 'reality' and 'fantasy'. From *Sirènades*,
Éditions du Seuil, France, 1998. The image of
the man with the melon may be seen as derived
from his drawing done on location and shows
the way in which he plays with visual puns.

The Snail that Climbed the Eiffel Tower

Odo Cross · John Minton   Martin Salisbury

The Snail that Climbed the Eiffel Tower published by John Lehmann, London, 1947, 86 pp., 253 × 186 mm, white boards decorated with a 3-colour image by Minton, repeated on the dust-jacket. Made and printed by Lund Humphries. Seven full-page 3-colour illustrations, numerous b/w line illustrations throughout.

1947 was an exceptionally busy year for John Minton. As well as illustrating The Snail that Climbed the Eiffel Tower for publisher John Lehmann, he also produced drawings for Stevenson's Treasure Island[1] and for The Wanderer (Le Grand Meaulnes) by Alain-Fournier.[2] In August of the same year he set off with writer Alan Ross for Corsica to return with the drawings which formed the basis of the book Time Was Away,[3] which would be published the following year. Minton was perhaps at the peak of his powers at this time. He had been introduced to Lehmann by friend and fellow artist Keith Vaughan and through Lehmann would have been introduced to Paul Odo Cross. Cross was later to move to Jamaica where Minton would stay with him on his visit to the island in 1950.

The Snail was the only children's book that Minton illustrated. It is now scarce and expensive to buy if one is lucky enough to find a copy. There is no discernable stylistic change in Minton's approach to illustrating for children from that used in his other books of this time – he does not compromise his lyrical drawing in any way and the book is the better for that. It is printed letterpress, with a mixture of black and white vignettes and three-colour, full-page illustration, with illustrated boards and dust-jacket.

The three colours, black, rust red and turquoise green, are kept quite separate except for some over printing onto the black. With Time Was Away the following year, Minton would experiment much more with overlaying colours to create new ones – a process at which he became extremely skilled. Here, in The Snail, the rather haphazard registration of colours adds to the relaxed fell of the images.

The book is a charming, neo-romantic classic, full of familiar 'Mintonisms' – the winding paths, the Samuel Palmer moons, the elegiac reclining figures under heavily textured skies. The dramatic end-papers depict a scene from the story 'Sandy', the tale of a sickly boy convalescing in a seaside town. The boy becomes entranced by 'Talina', a mannequin from a slot machine on the pier. One night the pier catches fire

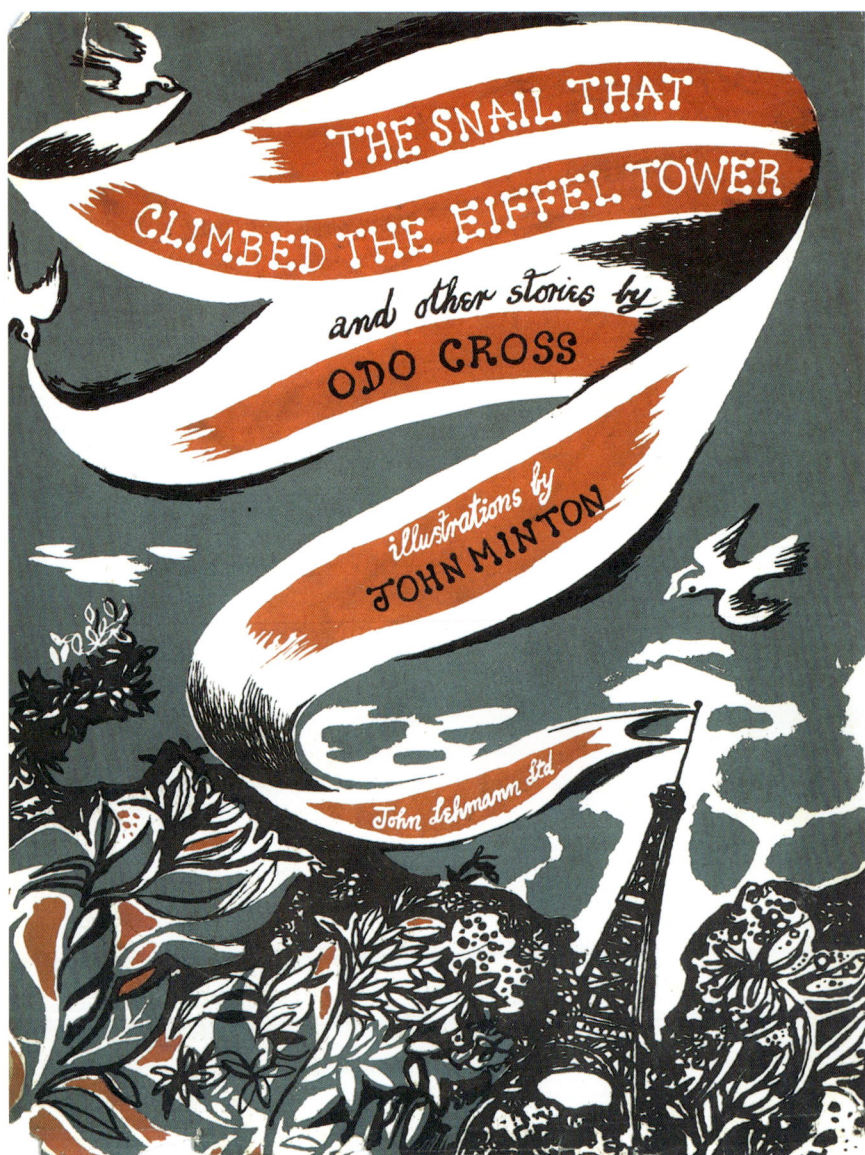

Front of the dust-jacket.

and the boy is distraught at the thought of the lovely Talina meeting her end. Some days later, the grieving boy discovers the mannequin washed up on the shore. 'Look', he says perversely, 'she's not burnt, only drowned.'

1. Camden Classics, published by Paul Elek, 1947.

2. Published by Paul Elek, 1947.

3. Published by John Lehmann, 1948.

Above: **two illustrations from inside the book.**
Below: **the endpapers.**

The Sixpence that Rolled Away

Louis MacNeice · Edward Bawden   Wendy Coates-Smith

The Sixpence that Rolled Away,
published by Faber & Faber,
November, 1956,
pp. 24, 210 × 154 mm,
white boards, decorated
from a lino-cut by Bawden.
Printed by Latimer Trend.
5-colour lino-cuts,
line-drawn title vignette and
6 illustrations. Dust-jacket.

The entry above was written by Barry McKay for the bibliography of *Edward Bawden* by Douglas Percy Bliss published by the Pendomer Press in 1979. *The Sixpence that Rolled Away* has tended to be obscured by the generally prolific career of Bawden and the rarity of the book itself, and very few references to it appear in print.

An enquiry to Faber and Faber brought this response from John Bodley:[1]

> I went to the archive this morning and the gist of what the file shows is that since we were (and are) MacNeice's publishers it was natural for him to offer us his story for children for publishing in England. The choice of Bawden was made by the production manager, David Bland, who would nowadays be known as the art director. Bawden had done plenty of work for Fabers before and it was an imaginative idea to commission him and let him choose the reproduction process himself.

> MacNeice liked the idea of Bawden doing the illustrations, and said when he saw them that he much preferred them to the American ones. Bawden was very pleased with the result, too, and did more work for the firm later. In a file is a letter from him telling Bland that *Graphis* in the 1960s was doing an article on his work, and that *Sixpence* was to be included.

> The book was more expensive than other books on the list at the time, and I cannot see that it was reprinted... The firm's policy in the field of books for children, then as now it was to publish the best things we could find. As the leading poetry house in the world we were especially pleased when one of our poets tried his hand at writing for children.

When I discovered that Louis MacNeice had written a story for children and that it had been illustrated by Edward Bawden I was very anxious to see it, and read it. But this is an example of an exceptional poet who lacks a natural instinct for fantasy writing for children. The book was published three years after Faber and Faber had published *The Magic Currant Bun* by John Symonds, but the vivid imaginative world made available to children by Symonds is missing here.

The ingredients for fantasy are in place but the fantastical vision which would transform and develop their potential is too thin, and rather laboured as a result. Where Symonds' characters gain a real purchase on the imagination and draw the reader into a fully realised fantastical world, MacNeice is content to display his characters engaging in an adventure on a technical level only – how to solve the problem. MacNeice's biographer Jon Stallworthy, makes no mention of the book and it has remained unknown

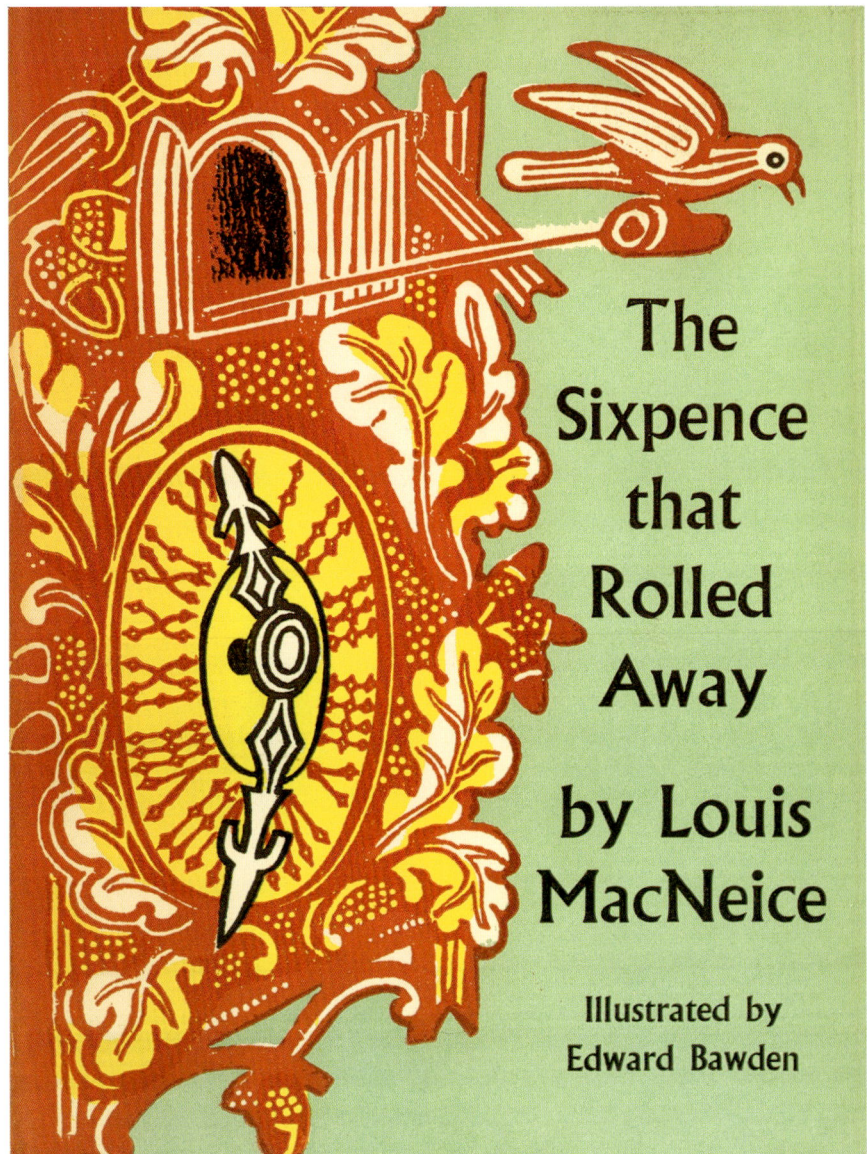

1. Letter to Wendy Coates-Smith, 27th January 2000.

Cover and inside pages describe the adventures of the mantlepiece community.

except to the fans of Edward Bawden. To Bawden, MacNeice's failure to rise fully to the challenge of writing for children is of no account. All that matters to him are the ingredients and the subject, and he shows how a master of visual fantasy can take limited material, invest it with real power and make it memorable.

The story features a community of objects which inhabit a mantelpiece. Disaster befalls the baby of a family of coins and notes, the Sixpence of the title, when it rolls over the edge of the mantelpiece and into the hole of the money-loving mouse below. The mouse is the villain, and wears bifocal glasses. She attempts to retain the chance acquisition of the Sixpence, and as the rescue proceeds, to add to this by keeping Dinah the half-crown and Bob the shilling. Eventually the coins are restored to the parents and everyone celebrates the happy ending by enjoying High Tea in the Money Box home.

Bawden created six four-colour linocuts and six black and white line drawings to illustrate the story.

The colour images are very powerful and provide at a general level the atmosphere required to bring the drama fully alive. At the same time his images delight

in the surreal elements of the community on the mantelpiece and project these as forcefully as anything he used lino-cutting to describe. Bawden reserves his line illustrations for the more direct needs of the action, and captures the bustling activity of the mouse in her hole as well as the desperate but ingenious use of the Indian Rope Trick to save the coin children.

But Bawden was a father as well as being an outstanding artist. His son Richard responded to some enquiries as follows:[2]

The Sixpence That Rolled Away must have given Edward great pleasure because the story and its humour is exactly in tune with his, and slightly surreal … It's odd that he chose to do black and white line drawings interspersed with coloured lino-cuts. The cuts were from one block, printed in different colours on different pieces of paper which were then cut up, put together like a collage, and then a bit of yellow and blue added with a roller which in places produced a crumbly gradation effect. He could cut a lino as quick as doing a drawing and he liked the crisp cut of the knife and the strong decorative quality it produced. At the time these were done he did the colour separations himself which meant each colour had to be done in black on each litho plate. The quality is so much better this way than colour half-tone separation.

Edward was quite childish himself and liked jokes about bottoms, and spiders, and creepy crawlies etc … Edward took a great delight in illustrating his letters to us and his friends with humorous scribbles, cats and cocktail parties etc. He felt freer doing this sort of thing particularly if there was a slightly cruel streak … His own childhood, being an only child, might have been more intense and inward. As a schoolboy at the Friend's School at Saffron Walden he was found pushing another head first down a manhole and punished by the headmaster who made him make a meticulous copy of a Victorian narrative painting. This might have been the initial push that **he** needed?

2. Letter to Wendy Coates-Smith, 20th February 2000.

A paper presented at the International Symposium, 'Art, Narrative and Childhood', Homerton College, Cambridge, September 2000

Art school and the children's book illustrator
Martin Salisbury

When asked at interview what they see themselves doing in four or five years' time, a significant number of applicants to the BA Hons Illustration programme at APU say, 'children's book illustration'. A growing number, in fact. Just a few years ago the majority (especially the boys) would be appalled at this idea, considering the area to be the height of uncool and synonymous with Postman Pat, Enid Blyton and Beatrix Potter. The arrival on the scene of such artists as Lane Smith, J. Otto Seibold and Sara Fanelli has changed all that, to the extent that few self-respecting 'cool' students will graduate without some examples of children's book illustration in the portfolio. This I think is a good thing, but I must confess that when hopeful applicants express these ambitions at such an early stage in their education I tend to experience a sense of foreboding. I suppose this is because I have found over the years that of the many graduates who have gone on to successful careers in the world of children's books, few were remotely interested in the area at the beginning of the course. Most, in fact, could be said to be in the 'no way' category. This while some, who professed an enthusiasm from day one, have found it difficult to get past the decorative 'fluffy bunny' stage.

These and other observations have led me to take a look at the way the children's book illustrator evolves and matures in Higher Art Education today, and in particular to ask what role drawing from life plays in this process. In the course of musing on this subject I revisited the thoughts of two much-loved twentieth-century illustrators, Edward Ardizzone and Lynton Lamb.

In the late 1950s Edward Ardizzone expounded his views on the 'born illustrator' in a talk given to the Double Crown Club and in an article written for *The Private Libraries Association Quarterly*. Ardizzone wrote rarely on illustration, unsurprisingly given his prolific output, but when he did his views were forthright, dogmatic even, on what motivates the illustrator. These views were informed by his part-time teaching at Camberwell and the Royal College of Art. His opinions apparently caused much controversy and debate among the designers, illustrators and printers who make up the membership of the Double Crown Club. He said: 'There are two things that all born illustrators have in common. The first is that their creative imagination is fired by the written word rather than the thing seen; the second is that when it comes to their illustrations, they would rather make them up than have recourse to life. In fact, as a rule, they don't like drawing from life at all... It might be truly said that the born illustrator is not very interested in life as it is. He likes to create his own version of the world around him. Actuality is not pointed enough for him'.

Ardizzone went on to talk about the relationship of image to text, the importance of illustration as more than a pictorial comment but an analogous visual counterpart to the written word. He championed the practice of copying (i.e. the work of 'good masters') as the most important part of the illustrator's training, and relegated the role of drawing from life to one of occasional sorties into the real world to confirm or 'sweeten' knowledge. 'Above all', he said, 'the born illustrator is an empirical artist. He likes to produce work by a method of trial and error on the paper, drawing a thing over and over again until it looks right, rather than finding a model and copying it.' The text of the talk was reproduced in *Motif* number 1.[1]

In *Motif* 2 another popular illustrator, Lynton Lamb, responded with an article titled 'The True Illustrator' in which he gently takes Ardizzone to task implying that he (Lamb) himself did not work in that way. Claiming not to be a 'born illustrator', he declares: 'I do not work directly out of my head but from copious notes.' He cites Rembrandt and Goya as 'superb illustrators' who were equally at home when working away from or in front of the model. 'As I see it', he says, 'whether one works out of one's head from memory and from recollected precepts, or works from notes and studies collected "ad hoc", the important thing is the transmutation of artifice or fact to a moment of dramatic truth.' Endearingly – to those of us who work as illustrators today – he manages to include a side-swipe at the people who commission illustration who, he says, 'have no real idea of how artists work'.

All of the images reproduced here were executed by the artists while studying for BA (Hons) Illustration at APU Cambridge.

1. *Motif*, a journal of the visual arts, edited by Ruari McLean, published in 13 issues between 1958 and 1967 by The Shenval Press.

Pam Smy, interior study, the illustration studios, Ruskin Building. Pencil drawing.

2. Oxford University Press, 1962.

Lamb was shortly to write the excellent *Drawing for Illustration*[2] (still one of the best books on illustration written by an illustrator) in which he was to look into these issues in greater detail, for example the importance of thorough visual research and the dangers of neglecting the disinterested study of nature. 'Those who rely on their visual memory may be betrayed by it', he says. Lamb and Ardizzone both felt it important not to 'draw down' to children. 'I do not believe in a "way" of drawing that is especially suitable for children', says Lamb, 'the idea of it comes from trying to separate the insight from the means of expressing it' ... 'let us remember that grimaces and runaway ponies do not make the whole story for children. The sun also shines on the nursery wall; a cold light is reflected from snow at the bus stop; the wind waves tall grasses in the meadow; the cat stalks in the shrubbery. Children understand this magic as well as any other' ... ' '...persons who adopt a special tone of voice when speaking to children often get what they deserve – a bored or embarrassed attention'.

Lamb's route to the profession of illustration was,

Sketchbooks
Clockwise from
top left: two by
Judy Boreham;
Portia Rosenberg;
Jane Simmons;
two each by
Pam Smy and
Sarah McConnell.

Jane Simmons.
Right: **Musicians.**
Below: **Fête.**

The issue of drawing – its importance or otherwise, its role in illustration – refuses to go away. It rears its ugly head in the context of many Art and Design disciplines but here I am concerned with the role of drawing, more specifically drawing from life, in the development of the children's book illustrator, or perhaps I should say the artist who chooses to work within that field.

Today's illustration students inhabit a world in which imagery bombards them from all directions; two-dimensional, three-dimensional, moving, digital, Photoshop and so on. It is therefore not surprising that for some the first instinct on arriving at university (especially in the fee-paying age with the attendant pressures from parents) is to say, 'OK, I'm here, teach me the tricks', their perceived idea of an illustration course being a programme where the secrets of illustrative drawing and computer techniques are revealed. This problem can be compounded by the modular system of subject delivery (a module being a block of time or period of study devoted to a particular area of learning) where learning outcomes must be defined in advance in terms of 'on successful completion of this module a student will be able to…'

This ethos of gradual and even skills acquisition does not always sit comfortably with the widely varying learning curves and needs of individual student artists. The temptation to write 'on successful completion of this module students will be able to … feel completely bewildered and left with more questions than answers but in a way which is likely to be of long-term educational benefit' has so far been resisted. Nevertheless, this 'compartmentalisation' of learning has to be carefully offset by regular tutorials where the individual student's work is looked 'holistically'.

The contemporary 'visual bombardment', I think, makes the teaching of drawing, and consequently 'seeing', more difficult, and more important than ever. It seems to me that it is far harder now for a student to

of course, very different to that of Ardizzone. He trained as a painter, Ardizzone worked for some years as a clerk whilst attending evening and weekend drawing classes. It is perhaps not surprising that there is a sense of the aristocrat versus the self-made man in the tone of their mild disagreement about the way illustrators learn.

Of course the world has changed somewhat in the forty-odd years since these views were expressed, but it is surprising to note how many of the issues continue to preoccupy those of us involved in the teaching of illustration. Most illustrators at that time emerged from a training in either painting or graphic design. In the last twenty years numerous courses specialising in illustration have sprung up and, of course, a far greater proportion of the population generally now has access to further and higher education. The pendulum swings regularly, and more recently in art schools the subject of illustration has often been moved around and hidden under various amorphous headings such as 'Graphic Communication' and 'Image Making'. Meanwhile, the 'born illustrator' quietly gets on with it regardless.

They both blushed. They both stuttered. They both stared at each other's feet. For some minutes there was a desperate silence. Then Norma spoke in a tiny voice.

'I like your shoes.'

There was more silence. Nelly gleamed pinker still. She tried to think of something to say but nothing came. The seconds passed. Then, suddenly and magically, she heard herself saying,

'Thank you. I like yours, too.'

Spread from *Norma No Friends*, by Paula Metcalf. Produced as third year Major Project. Published by Barefoot Books, 1999.

distinguish between the 'real' world and the world of received imagery. The student is more likely now than in Ardizzone's time to believe that she knows how to draw, for example a cow or a tree, when in fact the apparent familiarity has come in all probability from a variety of second- or third-hand sources that may include Walt Disney, TV, photography, children's books, etc. Speaking about the typical habits and behaviour exhibited by the 'born illustrator' species at Art School, Ardizzone observes, 'These same boys and girls have to be driven into the life class or out to draw something in particular.' No change there then. It is somehow reassuring to know that this battle to encourage illustration students to look at 'life' has been going on for some time (though Ardizzone rather cleverly suggested that it is not life that gives the illustrator his ideas but living).

Of course drawing is, or can be, about a great deal more than simply learning what things look like. In the education arena the subject of drawing tends to be talked about in terms of 'skills', which is always misleading. Those Foundation Art course exercises where students are forced to draw with their left or non-natural hand invariably produce the most acutely observed results.

In my experience, those students who have subjected themselves most fully to the often humiliating rigours of observational drawing have, with one or two notable exceptions, been the ones best equipped to go on to successful careers in narrative and sequential illustration. This process of looking, learning to see, has to be allied to an almost unhealthy interest in human nature and behaviour. I think it was Ronald Searle who, when asked what he would like to have been had he not been an illustrator, replied, 'a professional voyeur'.

To this end, students studying illustration at APU Cambridge are encouraged to draw, rather than to illustrate, for as long as possible. Drawing takes place in the context of trips abroad (e.g. Hungary, Portugal, Paris, New York), visits to local destinations where people congregate – swimming pools, parks, creches, places of work, e.g. factories, science parks, etc. These may take place as group or individual assignments. Through drawing and through observing, students explore their own individually unique 'take' on the world around them. Their responses may be humorous, serious, romantic, panoramic, obsessively detailed or wildly experimental and, of course, they learn far more from each other than they do from us. Whether or not the more studio-based work they are engaged in towards the end of the course is executed through traditional 'drawing-based' media is irrelevant, the experience of looking will have the same value, in breaking down preconceptions and discovering a personal visual language. What Ardizzone described as 'the practice of really looking at things and trying to commit them to memory' is also encouraged through the keeping of visual diaries, notebooks and sketchbooks. I would like to think my approach to teaching the subject is closest to that recalled by the American illustrator and author Tomie de Paola in *Children's Books and their Creators*.[3] He remembers a fellow student asking one of the instructors, 'When do we learn about style?' The instructor replied, 'We won't learn about style. Style happens naturally. If you keep working, eventually the way you can and want to express yourself will surface. Meanwhile, do the assignments, listen to the critiques, don't miss your drawing classes, painting classes, design classes and by all means, look at everything. Go to the galleries and museums. Your own style will surface.' He goes on to quote the words of another instructor, Richard Lidner, who told the students: 'Observe what you are interested in. Observe what kind of objects you surround yourself with. That will give you the clue to your own vision.'

3. Edited by Anita Selvey, Houghton Mifflin Co., Boston and New York, 1995.

Quentin Blake

Jane Stanton

Quentin Blake OBE is perhaps the only living British illustrator who can quite seriously claim to be a household name. In 1999 he was appointed the first Children's Laureate. The exhibition he curated at the National Gallery 'Tell Me A Picture' opened in February this year and has been visited by as many as three thousand visitors in a day. His book Words and Pictures published by Jonathan Cape was published last year and is an account of his career as an illustrator.

The book was dedicated to the Royal College of Art and it was there that I first met him as a student in 1981 when he was head of Illustration. He has been a source of inspiration and guidance ever since.

Cover of Words and Pictures Quentin Blake's autobiography. A Tom Maschler Book, published by Jonathan Cape, London, 1998.

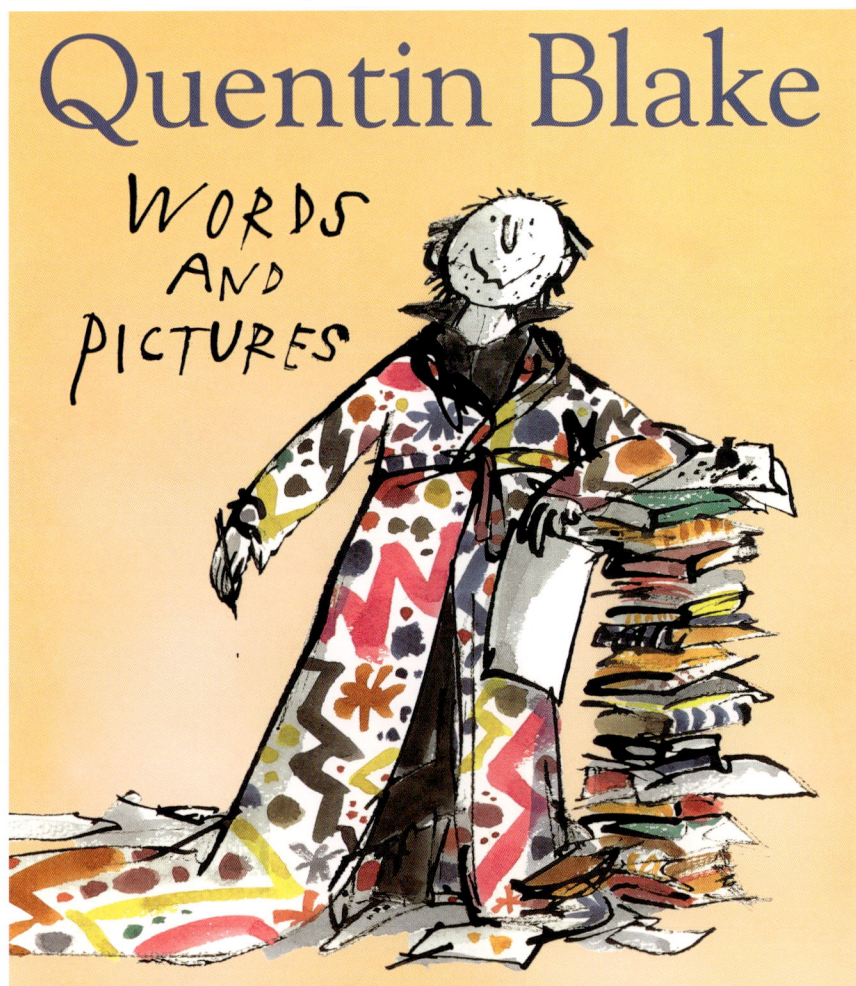

The interview took place in his studio in central London on an early spring day with the sound of gardeners at work on the magnificent trees in the gardens opposite. The large airy studio had a distinctly French feel and an air of organised, elegant chaos.

What has it been like as the first children's Laureate: has it been an intrusion or stopped you from working?
It wasn't at all as I expected. It has stopped me from working but I haven't minded. Before it started I wrote quite a few concerned letters (about the requirements of the role) but as soon as they rang up and said 'it's you' I think I reverted to being a sort of teacher or tutor and started thinking of things that I could do. I felt that if they were going to have a children's laureate that it was no good if people didn't know about it, I realised that I would have to do talks and lectures and visits just to get it visible.

I was asked to do a book The Laureate's Party and talks. Then I put forward the idea of the National Gallery exhibition and then the Bury St Edmunds exhibition. It's called 'A Bakers Dozen' and is a children's book exhibition with a dozen illustrators from your sort of generation and younger, Emma (Chichester Clark) Mick Manning and so on. I am the only veteran, a benevolent figure in the background. I have done three books this year that I perhaps wouldn't have done otherwise. It's crystallised things. You've got this kind of sheriff's badge that says you can do things. The National Gallery show for example, it wouldn't have occurred to me to think that I was in a position to suggest that otherwise.

Did you have anyone to refer to?
There have been grumbles in the past about
Poet Laureates and what they do and don't do.
No not at all, that's the marvellous thing about it. The thing I was most apprehensive of was that I would be working to someone else's scenario. Other people on the list were worried about this too but by the time I was appointed it was established that you would do whatever you felt was appropriate. In fact I have just received the sort of formulation for the next award in

Drawing of the studio from *Words and Pictures.*

May and it says you don't have to do anything at all if you don't want to! I have enjoyed it tremendously... doing my book and especially the National Gallery exhibition, it has turned out to be so interesting.

And the National Gallery exhibition, they were knocked out by the amount of interest.
Oh yes, their group visits were fully booked before the show started. I could hardly credit it. I thought that it wouldn't be reviewed very much but Bill Packer did a nice article and it was mentioned in the *Sunday Times* by Waldemar Januszczak, he wrote a long article about Brassaï and then at the end he said 'my children *made* me go and see this' and enthusiastically recommended it.

Did you have lots of time to yourself at home as a child?
I think I probably did (*his brother was ten years older and so he was virtually an only child*) and remember that this was during the war and so I suppose I listened to the radio. There was no television and we didn't go out all that much. I went to the cinema, I had friends in the street. I probably did have quite a lot of time. Not long ago I had a letter from someone who had been a friend of the family, she was reminiscing about the war, she was brought by her parents to see us and I think I was about eight. Somebody had said 'You'll find that he doesn't talk much but he draws a lot.' That must have been nearly sixty years ago.

Drawing of the studio from *Words and Pictures.*

The Owl Fancier Man and Woman, from *Words and Pictures.*

The Development of Miss Trunchbull, from *Words and Pictures*.

Going back to your early ambitions as an illustrator, was drawing and painting something that happened at home on a regular basis? Was it a visual or 'arty' house?

No no not at all. Nothing. I drew at school, I drew at home and then when I got to secondary school the husband of the lady who taught us Latin was both a cartoonist and a painter so once a term when I was about fourteen I used to go round and see him taking my drawings with me. Tobacco ash would fall out of his pipe onto the drawings. It was good because he talked about it as an art. He knew about serious drawing and painting. He was quite a good painter and a sort of cultivated chap, he was always playing the violin when you arrived. We talked about sending drawings to *Punch* and we talked about Michelangelo in the same breath.

You mentioned in your book that you went into a kind of apprenticeship, learning to be an illustrator as you went along. Do you think it was a better way of learning than going to art school?

I don't know. I've never regretted it although I have never decided whether it was the best. Now having been in an art school and taught in an art school I think that what I did in the end was to get a kind of correspondence course. I got most of the things that a student in an art school got eventually but it took me ten years instead of five.

I became part time at Chelsea where I did two days a week and that's where I did my life drawing because even though I was publishing drawings I didn't know how to do them. I felt I had to do life drawing and that was good because in a way you weren't forced to do it, you just knew that you couldn't manage without. When I met Brian Robb he would give me a tutorial about what I'd done; I remember taking him a lot of linocuts and drawings and he just turned them over one by one because he was seeing this sort of thing all the time.

You studied English Literature at Cambridge. This combination of words and images is really you isn't it? A lot of illustrators are passionate about English Literature. It's a very natural combination of interests.

Yes, absolutely. Often it's just a case of working out something that will do as a balance. I mean I did it partly because my school was able to prepare me to get into Cambridge and no doubt I could have got into an art school but it seemed like an opportunity that I didn't want to pass up really and I can remember thinking that I might stop reading. I thought that when I left Cambridge actually.

When I first met you at the Royal College I remember thinking that words really mattered to you and when for example we students were searching for a title for an exhibition you were always guaranteed to come up with just the right form of words.

Oh yes, yes, yes... I'm still doing it! Yes it's funny you don't notice that from inside but yes, it's true but it's a question of a balance between the two.

I think actually that teaching at the RCA also replaced some of what I hadn't had as a student because the problem with doing it on a part time basis is that you don't get that range of friends and acquaintances. When you leave you don't know other people that are supporting you, you don't have friends that have gone off to become art directors and that sort of thing so you haven't got that kind of network or hammock of support which is supplied by friends. A large part of my artistic acquaintance is from people like you, you know, a lot of them are ten or twenty years younger than I am. I didn't get those until I went to teach at the RCA, although most people get them when they are art students.

He went to look in the kitchen.
Hortense the cook was there,
boiling an egg for his breakfast,
but there weren't any cockatoos.

Cockatoos, published by Jonathan Cape, London, 1992. Hortense the cook in the kitchen.

Which particular books or art did you like as a child?

When I was a small child say five or six, I didn't know the names of any illustrators or anything. I knew the pictures and liked some but not others and then when I got to secondary school then I started remembering them. Just when I was leaving school in 1951, before doing national service I went to the Festival of Britain and I can still remember the pictures that I saw. They were by people that I knew already; Graham Sutherland, Edward Bawden, John Minton, Keith Vaughan, those sort of neo-romantics. There were two paintings, one by John Minton, one by Keith Vaughan and the John Minton was disappointing, it was a mural that was too much like an illustration somehow. He hadn't adapted, whereas Keith Vaughan, who used to work in a similar way, that Samuel Palmer watercoloury sort of way, had done something that was really a painting. I remember thinking, oh he's improved! So obviously I had some sort of a backlog of aquaintance and I think that most of the drawings that I had done when I was at school were influenced by people like that; with Picasso at the back of it.

A special distraction 'of the worst kind' as Quentin put it, was arranged as a plate of delicious French biscuits were offered and munched whilst we continued the interview.

He then told me that in fact his favourite illustrated book as a child was the Chicks' Own Annual and showed me a copy of the 1937 edition — a jolly comic strip collection of tales about the adventures of a band of assorted pigs, chickens and ducklings, some with rather unfortunate names.

You did a Postgraduate degree in Education. Do you think that's where you get your understanding of how children think or do you just remember what it was like yourself?

I think there are two things; the advantage of teaching experience is that you think about the book in relation to the people that are looking at it. If you are doing a lesson you are not just reciting information, you're setting up some kind of situation which elicits reactions from the people that you are talking to. Books do that, so that you know that you've got to retain their attention and that they're going to think something and you're going to say … and that's where that business of sequencing and matching up or not matching up words to pictures comes in.

So that's the social situation. The other thing is that it's a form of imitation like a form of acting because it's not from observation of children. Obviously I do see them but I don't do it on purpose and I don't draw them and I don't even think it's remembering, you know some people have very clear memories of their own childhood and I don't. Perhaps I do unconsciously but it's more like trying to imagine again if you were that thing in the same way that if you were imagining you were any body else in any of those books; say if you were trying to imagine that you were a society woman or a crochety old man, a dog or a witch – it's the same exercise.

Clown, published by Jonathan Cape, London, 1995. Helping with the housework.

Isn't it one of those things that artists often seem to hang on to, that childlike quality a kind of last vestige of something that most adults have lost and that acting thing is part of it.
Yes … something that you've failed to eradicate!

Do you regret not having any children of your own? To appreciate your work or even to refer to?
I don't. I've never missed that or regretted that. I think that is more important to writers than it is to artists strangely enough. I may be wrong but I think that writers write books for children in a way that artists don't. I mean I'm sure that if they have children they draw for them but very often writers really are writing about their childhoods and their own lives in some way and I think that the relationship with picture books and with illustration is different, I think that you are more inclined to 'key in' to other texts and other things.

Images of family life in your books are so well observed and touching. I'm thinking of the Dancing Frog where the mother is lying back in the chair drinking cocoa and the little girl is talking to her, it's so well observed it

almost looks as though you have done it from life but you haven't. Where do you get that sort of memory from?
I don't know, I think it's one of those things … it's hard to say without sounding pretentious there are ways of picking up stuff that you do almost without thinking about it. Think of Posy Simmonds and the amount of social recording that she is capable of doing, she cannot sit and write that, once she notices it she must have 'got it' if you see what I mean.

I remember reading something about George Eliot and somebody had asked how she knew about this religious sect she'd written about and she said 'well I was visiting somebody once and I was crossing the landing and the door was open and they were having a meeting in there'. Now that's not the research, but obviously she had picked up something. Even if you are someone whose experience has not been very far ranging or exotic you still get an awful lot of experience don't you? It just sort of beds down. It's being able to make use of it really.

You keep mentioning the 'ecstacy of being' and 'the pleasures of being and doing' a lot in your book and nearly all your drawings are like this, they are celebratory aren't they?
Yes, even though I don't necessarily spend a lot of the time being joyful!

It's quite interesting to me. I mean without making it more important than it is, it's something that the visual arts are good at, you know, and people don't talk very much about what visual arts are good at. Anything that comes under the heading of celebration doesn't get talked about very much because there's not much to write about in it. I mean it's better if you've got angst, dismay, despair, personal division, antagonism and so on. It's easier to write about El Greco than it is to write about Veronese, although I think that Veronese is a much more important painter really. A lot of his work is really a sort of celebration of vision almost, but this never quite gets the same value somehow as distress. Of course there are some ways in which distress can be more profound…

Celebration is harder to write about because what do you say? It's wonderful isn't it?

I remember some years ago, a crowd of us being in a Paris restaurant on one of those Royal College of Art visits, you being persuaded to do an act, pretending to be … do you remember?
Yes! Yes! either a parrot or a frog.

I remember someone saying at the time, that your act was just like one of your drawings! It brings me on to ask about the filmic and theatrical side of what you do. People often seem quite surprised about the relationship. When you start explaining the mechanics of making a piece of work, the acting bit is very important to you isn't it?
I think so and it's always interesting to me. I would love to do it though I'm not sure that I am temperamentally suited and I wouldn't be able to remember the words,

THE GREEN SHIP
Quentin Blake

Cover of *The Green Ship*, a Tom
Maschler Book, published by
Jonathan Cape, London, 1998.

The Green Ship Playing deck quoites
with Mrs Tredegar.

but the idea of it is fascinating. Last year when I went to a book fair at Aubagne near Marseille and I was set up to do a 'double act' with Claude Lapointe. Do you know him? French illustrator. He illustrated the *War of the Buttons* and he draws in a very economical but naturalistic way, you can see how everything works. His drawings you could imagine to be the opposite to mine and yet a lot of what we had to say about the job was the same, about the way you stage things, people's reactions and so on.

I think, particularly if it's somebody else's story it's a form of interpretation or transferal of ideas into a physical form.

You mention amongst your influences: Buster Keaton, Beckett, Conrad, all from many sources theatre, films, literature and so on. It's quite important for an illustrator to have a lot of influences isn't it?
Yes, it's the same as I feel about children's book illustration because you don't want it all to be tidied up. You don't want it to be a special little craft which you do in this way and it's not like anything else, because it's pictures of people doing things.

You describe your working process as having 'calm intervals of reflection' doing the basic design to the 'hairy bits' where it seems like you'll never find a solution. Do you ever fail to find a solution now?
Well, no no, ha ha. I always think it's like a veteran music hall comedian – there's always *something* that you can do!

You never totally fail but then some books are better

than others. I remember the *Just So Stories*: Brian Alderson said 'a lacklustre performance'. He liked the Kipling illustrations. Sometimes you get into something and it comes to life out of your hand and sometimes it doesn't, it's hard to tell.

The Folio Society once asked me if I would do more drawings for some Evelyn Waugh and I'd done two and I really didn't want to do any more, so I said 'it's all those men in suits that I'm not really good at, what I'd really like is a bit more dressing up, like the Hunchback of Notre Dame:' and they rang up and said "What a good idea". I'd never read the book! Actually getting going on that was very hard work, one of the things that helped to crack it was deciding that the pages could bleed, I don't know why; they were full page vignettes before. Somehow it helped the atmosphere.

In a previous edition of *Line* journal the American illustrator Marshall Arisman said that in the USA Illustration was a 'tainted' word and that it suffered from 'a hierarchy of purity' in comparison to painting and sculpture, do you think that this is the case in this country?
It's one of those questions that I find very hard to answer. I remember talking to Brian Robb about this and his saying that it's very difficult being being a painter *and* an illustrator. If you're an illustrator you'll find it harder to get on as a painter and I think he did to some extent. He did have exhibitions of paintings and I've never tried for that but I think it would be so. It's hard to quantify.

But Illustration and particularly children's book Illustration is so influential and perhaps for a lot of children it's their only real lasting contact with the visual arts.

Yes, and for the parents as well, that's the thing!

One of the ideas discussed recently at the Association of Illustrators has been that of a National Archive or gallery of illustration. There isn't anywhere very significant that you can go to look at a wide range of examples of the art of illustration and the history of it.

It would be a very good thing, but it couldn't live out of merely collecting work. It would have to be really positive in the way that it worked. It would have to have exhibitions and publications and a relationship with the public.

It would have to be retrospective as well. I'm very interested in late nineteenth-century illustrators: you mention Steinlen and a lot of people don't know who Steinlen is; if you think of Felix Vallotton people know a few paintings and they know prints by Felix Vallotton but they don't know the drawings he did in magazines. There's probably tons of other people.

I have got quite a lot of turn-of-the-century French humorous magazines like *Le Rire*, *Le Sourire* and *L'Assiette au Beurre*. You turn the pages and there's a drawing by Toulouse-Lautrec and that's probably the best drawing in the book and the most interesting.

There'll probably also be a drawing by Steinlen that will also be very good and a lot of other people working in a similar way because the whole atmosphere of what was going on was quite interesting. You see somebody like Lautrec and Bonnard and they're isolated but only because they're better than everybody else. You look at those pictures the women are all dressed as though they were drawn by what we think of as Toulouse-Lautrec, where as in fact a lot of people were doing very good drawings like this and it would be good to see them.

You see not many people know who Iribe is, do you know who Iribe was?

I must confess, no.

No, well there you are, when I was teaching at the college I had no idea, I wouldn't have known. I have got a book about him now, and he's in these magazines of mine. He started young, about eighteen, in the 1890s and he continually modernised himself so that he ran a magazine in the first war with Jean Cocteau called *Le Mot*, then he went into advertising and he became a furniture designer in the twenties, then he became a designer for Cecil B. de Mille and married Chanel at one point, but not for long! They're not hugely strong as drawings but brilliant on the page. The chance of anybody doing an exhibition of Iribe is very slight and yet it would speak to a lot of people I think. It's all part of the history of art.

You have started something now, having been the children's Laureate as an illustrator for the past two years. It would be nice to create a more permanent kind of thing wouldn't it?

Yes it would. I think that there are different ways that that could happen. I didn't think that being the Laureate was going to be as interesting as it has been. I thought because there's been a Poet Laureate for five hundred years it sounded a bit old fashioned and I didn't think it was the right title but it works for people, because it's something that's slightly outside the general run of things and I think it does work like that.

I've got a bit involved with the Campaign for Drawing and I've also got involved with a thing which is rather like what you're suggesting that is in fact a children's gallery of art and design, now that is art *from* children with art directed at children so there's quite a lot that could go on there and if that happens that would be the kind of thing that could also exist for adult illustration but it's got to be active. The French are trying to start something like this but I think they have merged the two together.

What projects are coming up next?

Well, the Laureate business officially comes to an end on May 16 when there will be a new one appointed. I will get back to doing my own work, I've got two picture books waiting and I need a decent run at those. Then there are one or two things that will be started if the National Children's Gallery of Art and Design goes forward.

I'm also helping to choose an exhibition for the British Council about contemporary children's book illustration which will start towards the end of the year and then tour.

Before we finish, what's your favourite book out of all those you have written and illustrated?

Well I've got one rather boring answer to that in that one of the things I like about it all is the variety of the work, other people's and mine. I liked it when quite by accident I did *The Green Ship* and *Zagazoo* in the same year and I liked that because they are treated in completely different ways. I mean you can't say *The Green Ship* is realistic but it refers to reality. *Zagazoo* exists entirely on the page, it just exists as drawings. I don't know... if I had to say one I think I'd tend to say *Clown* at the moment because it was a good example of telling a picture through stories entirely and the design and sequence of the book matters a lot, the pace of it matters, it all has to be in a sense 'acted' because you can't give any verbal account of it, makes me feel affectionate towards it, something like that... I don't know, gives it a slightly special place.

Lane Smith

Two spreads from *The Stinky Cheese Man & Other Fairly Stupid Tales*, John Scieszka and Lane Smith, Viking 1992.

"I have found a kernel of wheat," said the Little Red Hen. "Now who will help me plant this wheat? Where is that lazy dog? Where is that lazy cat? Where is that lazy mouse?"

"Wait a minute. Hold everything. You can't tell your story right here. This is the endpaper. The book hasn't even started yet."

"Who are you? Will you help me plant the wheat?"

"I'm Jack. I'm the narrator. And no, I can't help you plant the wheat. I'm a very busy guy trying to put a book together. Now why don't you just disappear for a few pages. I'll call when I need you."

"But who will help me tell my story? Who will help me draw a picture of the wheat? Who will help me spell 'the wheat'?"

"Listen Hen— forget the wheat. Here comes the Title Page!"

Title Page.

(for The Stinky Cheese Man & Other Fairly Stupid Tales)

PUFFIN BOOKS

"I planted the wheat. I watered the wheat. I harvested the wheat. Now do I get to tell my story?" said the Little Red Hen. "Say, what's going on here? Why is that page blank? Is that my page? Where is that lazy dog? Where is that lazy cat? Where is that lazy mouse? How do they expect me to tell the whole story by myself? Where is that lazy narrator? Where is that lazy illustrator? Where is that lazy author?"

My meeting with Lane Smith had finally come about. After a number of emails and phone calls it was agreed that I would drop in to his studio off Fifth Avenue in down town Manhattan, for a chat. As a long-time admirer of his work I was slightly nervous about meeting the great man, and as I stepped out of the elevator on the top floor of this elegant brownstone building and approached the door to his studio, my anxiety increased with the realisation that the image of him that had formed in my mind's eye had gradually morphed into Danny de Vito. This being my first visit to New York my visual imagination was clearly still handicapped by too heavy a diet of nineteen-eighties TV shows.

As Lane's friendly face and outstretched hand arrived at the studio door the stereotype was quickly banished and I stepped into a wonderfully spacious loft studio, the late afternoon sun streaming in on this warm spring day and the muffled sounds of the street drifting up from way below. An illustrator's dream studio if ever I saw one. Wall to wall books – a huge collection of contemporary and older children's books. 'Stuff' everywhere – film posters, a 'death mask' of Buster Keaton (acquired recently, I am later told), plants growing in the sunlight, toys, *objets*, etc., etc. I am shown into the room where he is currently working on the Mac, and where his wife, Molly Leach, who designs all of his books, works.

Lane Smith is a household name in America, thanks to the huge success he has enjoyed, both in partnership with writer John Scieszka (pronounced 'Shezka', I now learn), and through books of his own. His work on the film of Roald Dahl's *James and the Giant Peach* has also won great acclaim. He has twice won the *New York Times* Best Illustrated Book of the Year award and in 1993 received a Caldecott Honor. I try to stop myself from nosing around the studio too much, but Smith is a kindly host and we find many shared enthusiasms. He explains that he is working on the computer more and more at the moment, and has found it particularly useful with the new book (with Scieszka), *Baloney, Henry P.*, where he needed to create a kind of retro science-fiction feel. He is experimenting more and more with generating colour and shapes on screen alongside the scanning in of hand-rendered textures.

One of the things that impresses me most about Smith's work is the sense of synthesis achieved between illustrator, writer and designer – the common pursuit of 'bookness' ahead of individual egos. With Scieszka and Leach in, for example, *The Stinky Cheese Man & Other Fairly Stupid Tales* the characters are constantly interacting with the format of the book itself. 'Listen, hen,' says Jack the narrator, '...Forget the wheat. Here comes the title page!' And later in the book the hen looks across to the empty white page – 'Say, what's going on here? Why is that page blank? Is that my page?' It is anarchic and subversive yet clearly born of a love of books.

This sophisticated integration of concept/design/ typography/illustration must surely come from a very close working relationship between the three of them. I wondered whether such a book was conceived by all of them in a meeting aimed at the creation of a book. 'People are often surprised that the process is not quite as collaborative as you might think,' says Smith, 'though with *Stinky Cheese Man* it was more so than the others.' He goes on to explain that normally Scieszka will send a text and then Smith and Leach will work things out together. Smith says that Scieszka is great to work with, 'When we send him ideas, he will generally say "yup...great".' With *Stinky Cheese Man* it was different in that the three of them did talk about it much more together. Scieszka had taken the

manuscript to a publisher some time before (i.e. before the subsequent success of *The True Story of the Three Little Pigs*) and they had been very wary of the whole thing. After the *Three Little Pigs*' success it was more of a 'Yeah, fantastic, we love it' response.

Smith says that one of the great benefits of the success that he has enjoyed with Scieszka is the power that it gives him to take risks with his work. 'The good thing is, it's not a struggle any more to get published. I mean if I wanted to, I think I could take anything to the publisher and maybe they would say, well, this isn't going to sell so we are not going to give you any money... but I'm just happy that I have an outlet for my work, because there are so many folks who are trying to get published. It's very tough.' I asked whether this success was a long time coming.

'Well, oddly enough my very first book, called Halloween ABC, I took it to MacMillan and they

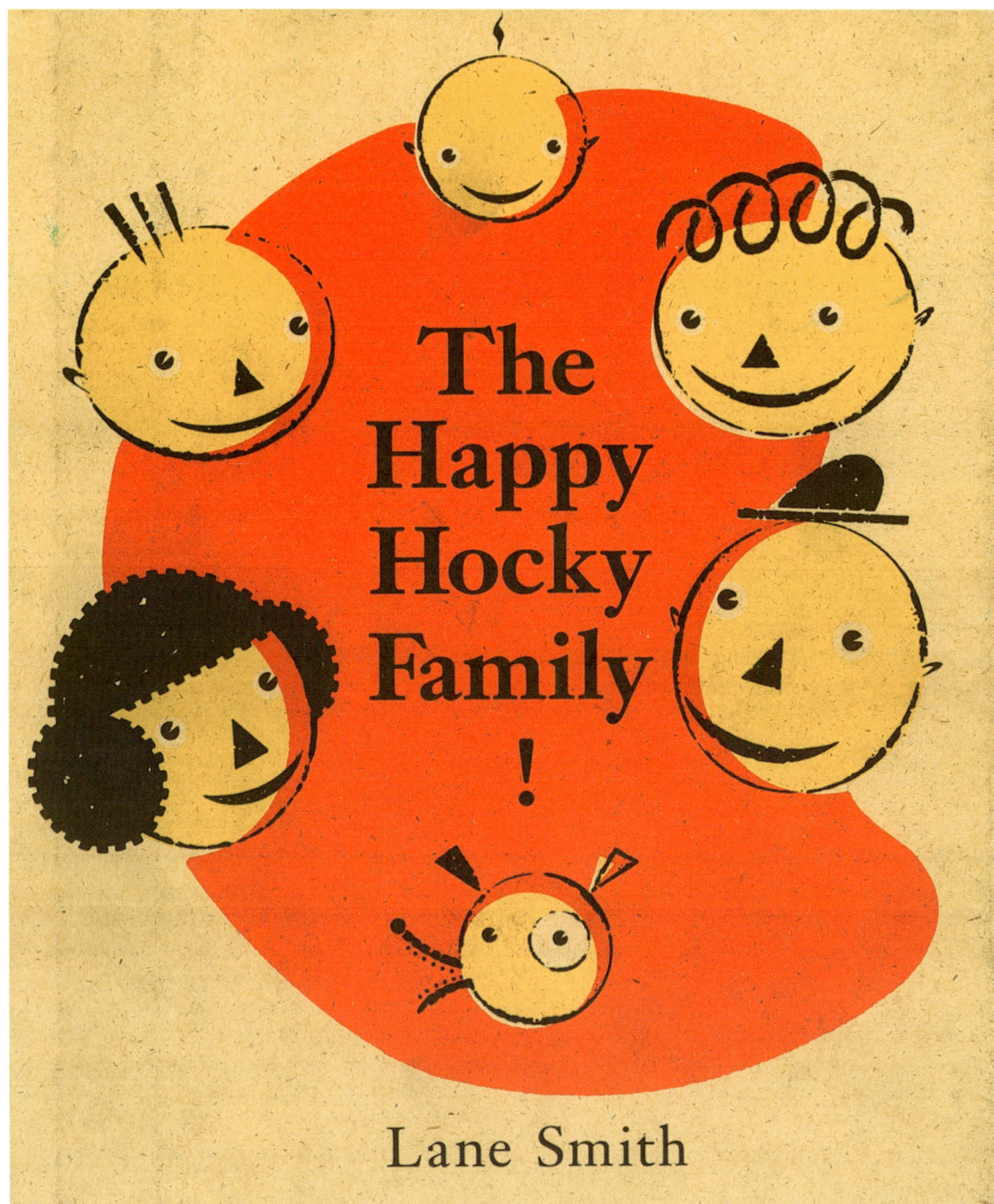

Illustrations from
The Happy Hocky Family.
Left: **front cover.**
Right facing: **inside pages.**

50

1. *The True Story of the Three Little Pigs*, John Scieszka and Lane Smith, Penguin, 1989.

2. Lane Smith, Viking, 1993.

published it. And then when Molly introduced me to John and we put together the *Three Little Pigs*[1] dummy no one wanted to publish it. I thought we should take it to my first publisher, but they didn't like it, and we kept shopping it around and finally we ended up at Viking and our editor there was also very tentative but she said, "OK", and they put out a few copies, and they sold, and they put out a few more copies, and they sold. In the end it kept going back to the press.'

I venture that it is sometimes difficult to have confidence in publishers when they seem so unsure themselves. Smith agrees. 'When we turned in *Stinky Cheese Man*, they liked the stories but were very confused again when we produced the finished book. They were afraid no one would like it. But they said, "We're going to trust you".'

One of my personal favourites of all Smith's books is *The Happy Hocky Family*,[2] which he wrote and illustrated himself. The book is an affectionate spoof of the American 'Dick and Jane' series with which Lane Smith grew up (as in our own 'Janet and John'). We look at one or two originals of this series from Smith's bookcase and laugh at a particularly amusing primer on world politics with its ocasional use of UPPER CASE words for EMPHASIS:

> Some countries don't elect their leaders but they give them GREAT POWER. This is fine if you happen to like the leader but NOT IF YOU DON'T.

Molly Leach has faithfully referred to this typographic approach in the design of *The Happy Hocky Family*. Smith says, 'I did that book, I think, after *Stinky Cheese Man* and it did pretty good. It sold about forty thousand copies which is good for a children's book, but nothing like the books that John and I do together. The books that we do together actually sell millions of copies so we're kind of united at the hip. Fortunately we like each other a lot, we get along great, so it's a good thing. But they built us up as a team so much... we each like to try something different when we do something on our own

or with another writer/illustrator. It's a chance to do something more esoteric, knowing that we're working to a smaller audience.'

Recent examples of Scieszka and Smith working independently of each other are the former's book with Dan Adel called *The Book That Jack Wrote* and Smith's collaboration with the writer George Saunders on *The Very Persistent Gappers of Frip*.[3] Looking at the cover of the Scieszka/Adel book I find myself reading out loud in my best New York advertising voice, 'Brought to you by the guy that gave you *The Stinky Cheese Man*.' 'A concession to the marketing department!' laughs Lane, 'I think they got a little worried it wouldn't sell. The publisher wanted to do the same with *Gappers* – release it in paperback and say on the cover, "Illustrated by Lane Smith, illustrator of *The Stinky Cheese Man*, written by George Saunders." I said, "No, no" and now they're not going to put it out in paperback at all because I made such a stink.'

The Very Persistent Gappers of Frip is a stunning book. I had not encountered it before my visit to Lane Smith's studio, and was delighted to find myself returning to England with an inscribed copy. However, the story of its publication is somewhat depressing. I had asked which of his books Lane was most proud of.

'Well, I think *Stinky Cheese Man* was our most ambitious, certainly for me it was the most ambitious that actually paid off. We put everything in there and everyone seemed to get it and it won awards. *The Happy Hocky Family* I'm very proud of – it reflects more my own individual sense of humour. Also *James and the Giant Peach*. But the Gappers book is kind of the apex almost of all that. I was able to put everything in there: mood, atmosphere, character. And we were able to do everything we wanted design-wise with the vellum cover and everything. But it's a BIG BUST! No one knows it's out there. I think it's a huge publishing catastrophe. They printed up something like 75,000 and they've sold 3,000.'

The book has been aimed by the publisher at the adult market. Smith feels this is a mistake. "It was completely mismarketed. It's perfectly appropriate for kids, there's no profanity or anything, and it actually has a nice moral and a nice message. But I guess they just assumed they could put my name on the cover and people would seek it out. And I said, "No, it's got to be in the kids' section." But no, so it's a big bomb, but I love it, and I love the writer, and I hope they let us work together again – but maybe not!'

Of course the situation is very much the same here in England and from time to time someone attempts to revive the tradition of the illustrated book for an audience other than children. A recent study day at the Victoria and Albert Museum addressed this very issue. I mention this dialogue to Smith and ask if the situation is similar in the States. 'Yes. Well, I knew there was a problem because right before this book came out I had read about Raymond Brigg's *Ethel and Ernest* and I couldn't find it anywhere. So I asked, "Would I find this in the adult section or the junior section or the kids' section or what?" And they went away to look it up on

the computer and I think it was under sociology or something. People don't know what to do with these books. And, Art Spieglemann had done *The Wild Party* for the same publisher which also did not do well – unlike *Maus* of course.'

'So anyway I thought maybe we'll get some luck. But we didn't catch any luck. But I still love it. It'll be like the *Happy Hocky Family* and five years from now people will say, "I love that Gappers book – I found it in a used garage sale".'

It is truly a book for the connoisseur, and I find I cannot contain my enthusiasm. Lane jokes, 'Why, thanks, that's two of us who like it!'

Moving on, we talk more about the actual techniques and processes involved in his work and he produces several pieces of original artwork from *Gappers*. Like many people (he tells me) I am surprised that the originals are not bigger. He works same size.

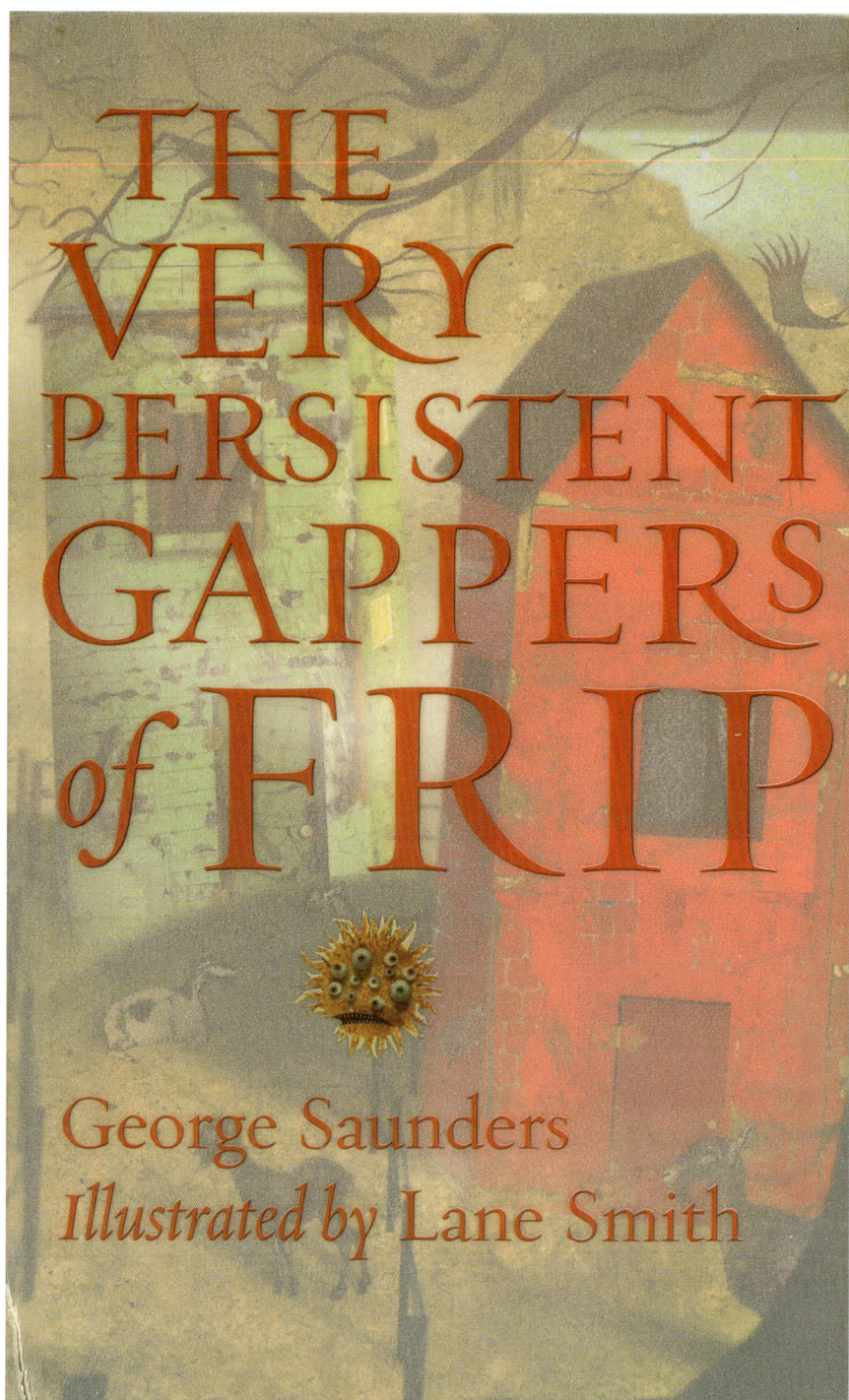

The Very Persistent Gappers of Frip.
Above: **front cover.**
Right facing: **inside spreads.**

3. George Saunders and Lane Smith, Villard Books, 2000.

● ● ●

IN THE HOUSE NEXT DOOR LIVED Mrs. Bea Romo, a singer, whose children, two sons, were also singers. They all sang in a proud and angry way, as if yelling at some- one, their faces bright red.

"It's a miracle!" Mrs. Romo shouted next morning, when she came out and discovered that her yard was free of gappers. "This is wonderful! Capable, dear, you poor thing. The miracle didn't happen to you, did it? I feel so sorry for you. God has been good to us, by taking our gappers away. Why? I can't say. God knows what God is doing, I guess! I suppose we must somehow deserve it! Boys! Boys! Come out and look!"

17

Then she went into her house and shut the door.

She made a fire and cooked the fish. She sat down with the plate of fish in front of her window. She watched the Romos and Ronsens swim back across the swamp and remount their houses. She watched Robert Romo's shoe slip off and fall in the muck. She watched Sid Ronsen sitting with his head in his hands, possibly weeping, and Carol Ronsen sort of consoling him, by pat- ting him on the back.

And she soon found that it was not all that much fun being the sort of person who eats a big dinner in a warm house while others shiver on their roofs in the dark.

That is, it was fun at first, but then got grad- ually less fun, until it was really no fun at all.

"Father," she said. "I guess we'll be having some company."

"What in the world?" he said. "Our house is so small, and there are so many of them. We have so little, and they'll use so much. This is a really big change. It makes a lot of extra work."

"Yes it is," said Capable. "Yes it does."

"But we're still doing it?" he said.

70

to two pair of
to Cash
to order
of Boots fine
goods from Brighton
of tobacco to Lyme
for repairing

Left: **illustration from** *Squids Will Be Squids*, John Scieszka and Lane Smith, Viking, 1998.

'Some people are disappointed when they see the originals because they assume they are big and textural like stucco walls, and they are in fact small and smooth – almost like transparencies. I just stumbled on this illustration technique when I was at school. I tried to preserve one of my paintings, and I sprayed it with acrylic spray varnish and the oil started bubbling up, but I liked it. So I experimented more with blow-dryers and things and here we are.'

I mention that I have spotted one or two Lane Smith impersonators around but generously he says he is not really conscious of it except when his mum rings up or sends a cutting through the post saying, 'This guy is ripping you off!'

'I used to be afraid people would spot my influences more. When I was in school I splattered a lot like Steadman.' 'Didn't we all?' I reassure him. In fact Smith's influences are broad and eclectic – fine artists such as Paul Klee and Kurt Schwitters, but perhaps more importantly the medium of film, especially the silent movie and in particular Buster Keaton.

I ask about his art school education and whether there had been any particularly influential tutors. 'Yes, I've always, throughout my life, been fortunate in that someone has sort of taken me under his or her wing. When I was in high school I really wasn't sure what I was going to do with my life. I didn't really know if you could have a career doing art and illustration, and my art teacher actually drove me to the art centre, an hour away in Pasadena, and set me up an appointment with counsellors. I'm the only one in my family who has ever gone to college. So I wasn't sure how to go about it. I hadn't taken any of my college prep tests or any of that. But then once I was in the art centre, around my third year, strangely enough, there was an advertising teacher, Brian Birch, who did really slick ads for Porsches and Campbell's Soups, and for some reason he really liked my work. I don't know if it was because it was good but it was just completely different from the other kids in the class who were doing the airbrush Porsches.' We reminisce awhile about those late seventies days of airbrushed naked ladies on motorbikes.

'Anyway, they were all doing this horrid stuff, but I think he really inspired me because he would hold my work up and say to the class, "You should be doing things like this." Up until that point no one had taken any notice of me. It was a little embarrassing but looking back it was probably just to shake everyone else up. But it was good because they could all draw much better than me.'

Smith does not do any teaching himself. 'No, I don't know if I'd be a good teacher', he says. 'If someone was struggling with something I think I would find it hard to lead them in another direction or to say what I really think. I hate criticism myself, when I was at school I had such a thin skin. In fact now I find it very difficult to be critical when I'm working with others. We are working on an animated TV series for public television here at the moment and I just got some sketches faxed this morning and I feel bad correcting everything and saying, "This is sloppy" and "The hands aren't right" and "Draw the carrot like this." I do it because it needs to be done but I hate it. I usually end up just redoing everything so, rather than criticise anyone, I do another drawing and say, "How about doing it like this?"'

I venture that it must be very difficult anyway handing your work over to someone to be animated in that way. 'Well, I love it when you hand it over and someone "plusses" it. Like with *James and the Giant Peach* – those animators were all top notch, and once the characters were designed, well, their animation was just great. It always came back more wonderful than I could have imagined. I guess we're talking about higher money brackets. With places like Disney you can just kind of "let 'em go".'

Working in film had been a logical step for Smith as a life-long lover of the medium, but at the moment he is taking 'time out' from it. 'Although I love film, and I think I'm pretty good at it, there's just too many people involved. I was directing the Stinky Cheese Man movie, which is now in turnaround, and I had 200 people working for me, and I had to meet with each one to explain things, look at stuff, go over storyboards and meet the writers. Then sit in on production meetings. It was about three years ago, it was a co-production, Nickleodeon and Paramount Pictures. Paramount wanted it aimed a little older, and Nickleodeon wanted it more like "Rugrats" – younger. And we were right in the middle. We had a really great contract and we were able to buy our rights back and we took it to Universal. Universal was fantastic. The Executive there was great – this guy Doug Wood. He used to be a stand-up comic, so he was just a normal guy and funny and a great writer, and he understood exactly what we were trying to do and so things were really moving ahead. And then the CEO got fired and a new guy came in the next day and killed off all five animation projects. He just canned them and said, Oh, you know – "not very cost-effective, so we're not doing any animations." So now we have the rights back and I'm not sure what we'll do. I'm kind of thinking I might like to do a short, maybe a little half-hour short for the cartoon network.'

Finally, I wondered whether Smith had any other long-term ambitions for his work. 'No, I think as I get older I get less ambitious. I did want to do more film work and direct more things, but I guess I'd like to do more fine art things – I just feel like doing some big paintings. But I wouldn't exhibit them or anything. I'd just do them for my house. I've always loved printed matter, and I've never had any desire to sell work in a gallery or anything. I haven't done any painting, working on canvas, since I was at school.'

I suspect that whatever Lane Smith turns his hand to it will exhibit the same high standards that are so evident in his corpus of work to date. It was time for me to leave. My host reminded me not to forget to call in at the 'Books of Wonder' children's bookshop nearby and to try to take a look at his favourite museum, the Forbes Museum on Fifth Avenue and 12th. I made my way back up Fifth Avenue enriched by my short meeting with one of the USA's finest contemporary illustrators.

I had done two other books in rough form all the way through. They just needed to be painted. But I wasn't happy with the stories, they didn't quite work.

I spent a lot of time on this one. It went through lot of changes. There is a cat in the book, but originally there was a little girl performing the same actions as the cat. I did six pictures with the little girl. I laid them on the floor and gave myself a crit. A little girl chasing a big man through the town by herself, but it's not going to work – socially it's not on. I got rid of the girl and kept the cat. While I was working on the book I was doing a lot of things at the same time.

The book had to work for me, and hopefully for children too. Coming from a background of work of a political or social nature, the imagery, just by nature of what I was doing, could be fairly dull and it was dealing with things in an entirely different visual way. I wanted to do something more joyful – more up. At the same time I had started working on the computer, which is a very big learning curve, just coming to terms with the actual machine – let alone using any programmes. It took about a year, just trying to work out different programmes and trying out different visualities. I kept on giving myself stern crits. I would pretend they weren't my work and just carve away. I started working with the pictures on the desk, just scanning them in because I was using the colour copier a lot to change colours around and cut things out of colour copies and collage these. I had thought that the computer would be like a bigger colour copier and that I'd remain working on the desk.

As things went on I found I was working more on screen and less and less on the desk and I found I could actually work straight to screen. What I hadn't realised was that the computer gave me immense possibilities working in layers. In one of the pictures there is a magician on normal sized roof tops, but because I had the computer I could dramatically change the scale and have a magician that fills the whole page on top of some very small roofs down at the bottom of the page which I wouldn't have thought of if I'd not had the computer to play around with. It is almost too much at

times because you can work at so many combinations, throwing this out, and the other because everything is on layers. In a way that's how I've always worked. When I worked at a desk with paper I would often tear one piece of image away from the corner area, and stick it down somewhere else. So the computer gave me this possibility ad infinitum.

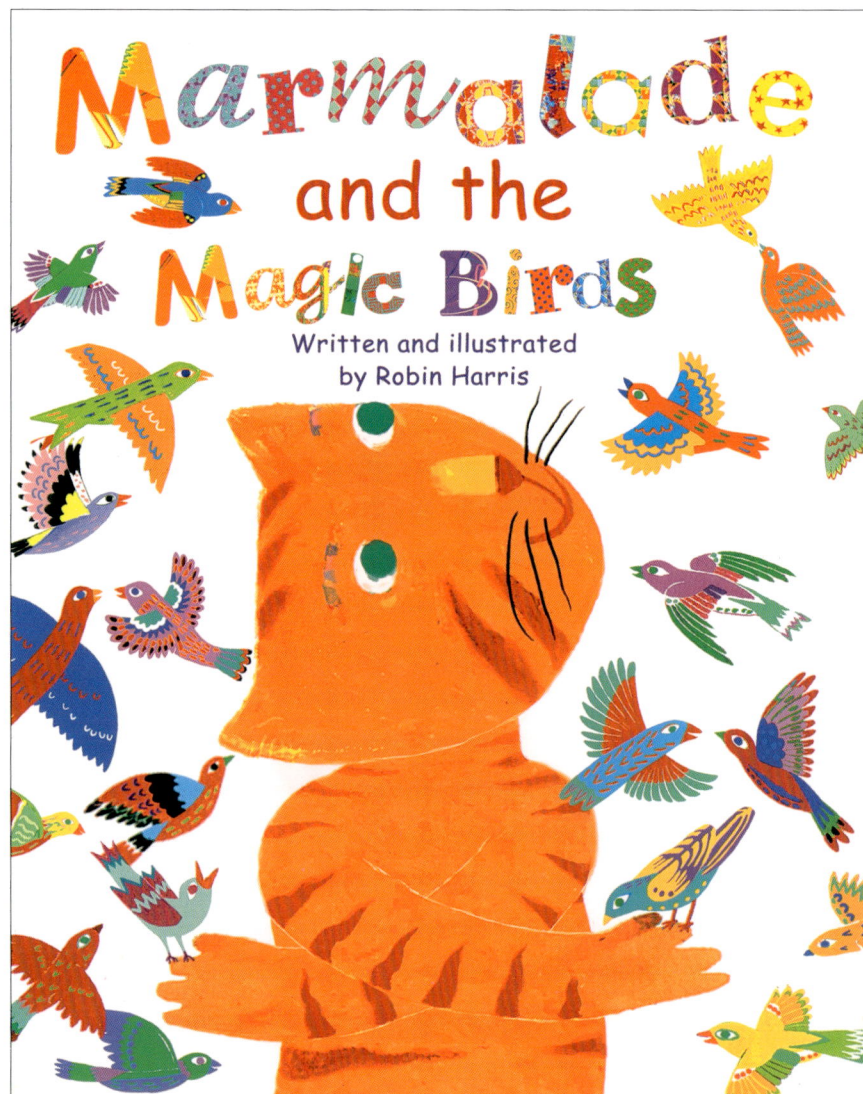

'Of course I can!' the magician replied. 'I am Ertax the Tanfastic, and I can do whatever I like! OM-POM-PUSH!'
'There you are!' cried Marmalade. 'Let those birds go!'

Cover and inside spread from *Marmalade and the Magic Birds*, **published by Barefoot Books Ltd, 2001.**

I started off on the desk and took some stuff to publishers. One in particular, who was very interested, asked me to make some changes to the book, but eventually said 'No'. I thought that it was a mistake to accept their visuality, to compromise what I thought and so as I was now working more on the screen I redid all the pages on the computer. When you are working you build up libraries of colours and textures.

I tend to use two programmes the most, Painter, which doesn't mimic what you do with real brushes and paints, but has its own remit. The problem with Painter is that its layering ability is very limited, so I tend to use Photoshop for that. In computer terms a layer is a sandwich – bread, meat, tomatoes, lettuce then bread. They just sit on each other, and if you have one figure on a layer, the rest of it will be transparent so you are able to see everything else through that layer – as though it were on a transparent cell. You can group a number of layers together. In the picture with the children leaving the theatre I had 98 layers in all because I tried different heads on different bodies. It was actually easier than to paint it, and I could get a better result because I could work it out and do all the changes.

The book gradually grew from a lot of different areas. I wanted to change my work, I began to use a computer, and then I wanted to work for children rather than adults – which actually changed what I thought about my work. I am very happy about it because several friends who have children of 5–6 have told me that the children really love it, which is the best criticism.

The story

Stories have to have an element of turning the page and an element of surprise. If you know the ending at the start, it doesn't hold you. I can remember as a child I loved intricate pictures. I liked to have an entire picture of a zoo or something and see all the different animals. I wanted value for money, and that has stayed with me. I found it more difficult than I'd thought to do a children's book. Actually, working out a story with a beginning, middle and end was hard. You can't really start the story half way through. You have to start with the hero or heroine and introduce them. You have to lead the reader through, with an identification with the character. I learned some things going round the publisher. For instance, when I first drew the cat, he had a long neck. But you have to do the cat as though it were a child, and imagine what a small child would look like in terms of the animal. The child needs to imagine themselves in that adventure, in terms of a cat or whatever. A lot of children's books do use animals rather than children because, in a way, they are safer.

Actually I didn't really get the idea of children's books until Val Pigeon said the word 'friendly'. This was a revelation for me, I just hadn't thought about it in that way.

Working with computers

In terms of the computer you just find out more and more what they can do. They are not something to be frightened of or get obsessed about. They are just a tool, and they can do amazing things and allow you to

After the show, each child took home a painted aeroplane.
Above them, the birds swooped and sang.

do a lot of difficult things. In today's day and age I feel easier knowing about them.

I use a Mac, at first a cheaper one – just to get the hang of it. But after a few months I got a more expensive one. If you are doing high-end visual work you need a lot of memory so you need to get the best you can.

Historically artists and graphic designers used Macs, but now these are lagging behind PCs in terms of megabytes, megahertz speed and various aspects like that. But there is something about the Mac which makes them more friendly. I think someone once said that working on a PC was like living at home with your parents, and working on a Mac is like having your own flat. PCs try to do everything for you. But you can actually change a Mac and make it work for you in the way you want it – but that is impossible with a PC. So even with the greater speed, I would still opt for a Mac.

What really got me into it was discovering that even when I was complaining about the machine and saying 'What a terrible machine!', but I came to the realisation that went it went wrong, I'd just forgotten something simple. So then I assumed that everything that went wrong was my fault – but the machine had a virus. So I worked all over Christmas and New Year trying to sort it out. I learned the actual machine – the extensions, the preferences, control panel, the Apple menu and the folders inside the hard disc and how they all went together. Doing this gave me a much sounder footing with the computer and when things went wrong I could generally sort them out rather than having to rely on someone else. I learned the simplest graphic

programme, Colour it, which didn't have any layers, just the basic brushes. Whereas something like Photoshop is too much. I don't use a mouse, it would be impossible. I use a tablet and a pen.

At first, just to get used to hand – eye coordination, looking at the screen but drawing on the tablet seems to be difficult, but after a while it comes very naturally. It was a very steep learning curve, and I learned very diligently a lot of programmes, because needs must.

Conclusion

Obviously before I got a computer I'd seen a lot of illustration and visuality which had been created on a computer. A lot of what I found looked a bit plastic and thin. I didn't like it and I was worried by that so when I could see the different effects and filters that you could use to jazz things up I determined that I didn't want that. I wanted to keep the same vision that I had on the desk, and I'm actually quite pleased that I have managed to keep that vision. I certainly went overboard when I first started using a computer. I see students who very easily succumb and begin to over-egg the pudding. I'm old enough to have the discipline to bring to the computer what I want, rather than just use it for effect.

The run of 1,000 copies of *Marmalade* has sold out, and I have a couple of new ideas. But now I know what makes a good book I am more critical. The story makes all the difference. You think as an illustrator that it is going to be the pictures, but when you get down to it the story is the main driving force – which came to me as a surprise actually.

Inside spread from *Marmalade and the Magic Birds*.

My first book using computers was *Rocket Countdown*, which I did with Walker Books. I wanted nice flat colours which seemed appropriate for the subject matter, which is just the story of the rocket flying up into space. I wanted it to be very flat and bright and it seemed absolutely appropriate to use a computer to do the artwork but I also really liked the combination of drawing in something very, very low tech like charcoal, and combining that with super flat, super efficient colours, so it was a little joke, drawing in something

Cover of *Rocket Countdown*, published by Walker Books, 1995.

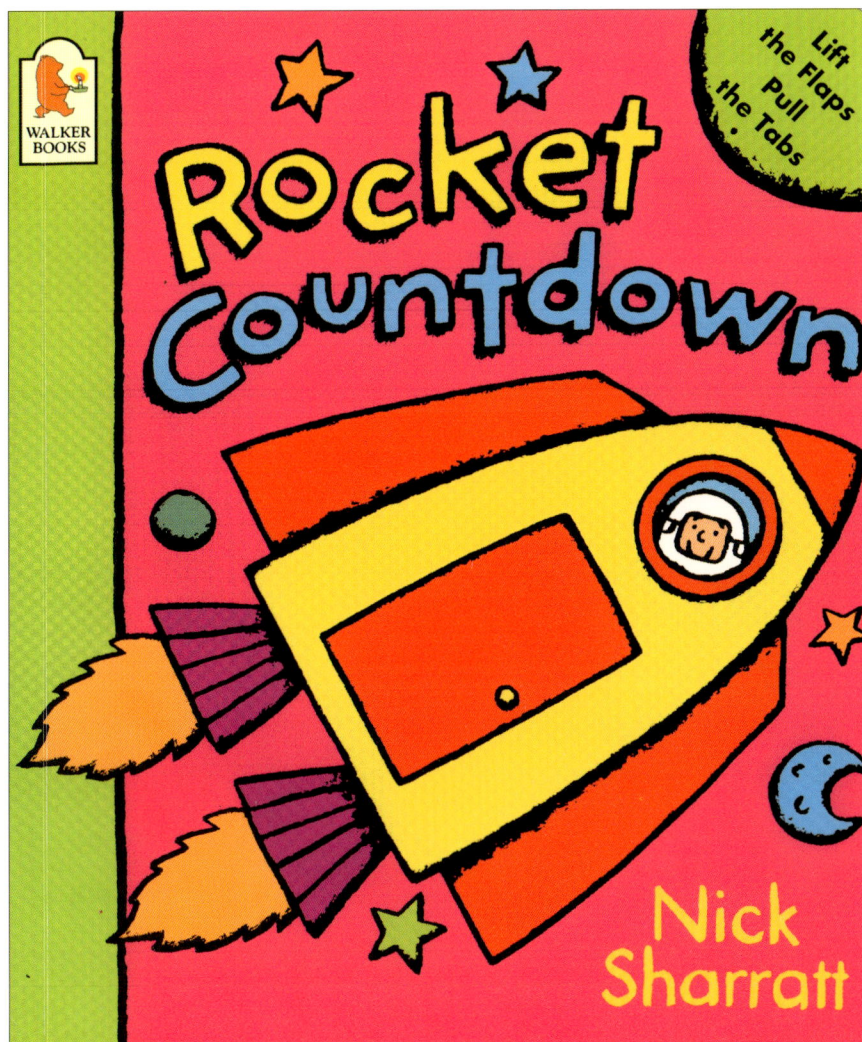

that you can't control at all and combining it with something that's super efficient and controlled. I never know what I'm going to get because I scan the charcoal line as a solid. It's always going to break up and some bits of the line are going to be thicker or thinner than you imagine.

The drawings were done to the same size as the printed book. So that was the first one and that was done in-house, I know nothing about computers at all so I always have to work with a technician. Nearly all these books have been done with the same guy, a guy called John Peacock with whom I now have a very good working relationship. This one was quite straightforward, it was just selecting seven colours, the brightest colours possible and then providing a colour dummy and letting them get on with it in-house. Then I was commissioned to do this series for OUP of baby books, and I wanted to do the same thing. I wanted to draw in charcoal in a naïve, almost baby-like way but combine that with very neat patterns and perfectly flat colour to give the impression of having done a collage, especially using little segments of simulated fabric or carpet texture or wood texture. All the patterns were made up.

I draw little templates and then we make repeat patterns from them, which is quite fun. So this has turned into a series. This first one actually was quite an ordeal, this was the first one where I went and worked with John and I sat beside him, and saw what was happening on the computer screen. I asked if we could have the pattern a bit larger or a bit smaller or whatever, and it was very, very time-consuming and also very frustrating when I finally got the first set of proofs because they were absolutely nothing like the images on the computer screen where I'd seen these lovely glowing colours. So it was a bit of a baptism by fire really and it had to be re-proofed and I also had to work out a better way of communicating with John so that we didn't waste time. It was a bit like the Golden Shot. I'd have cheeks on my characters and we would spend far too long, me saying could the cheek be a little bit bigger, a little bit bigger, slightly to the left or to the right.

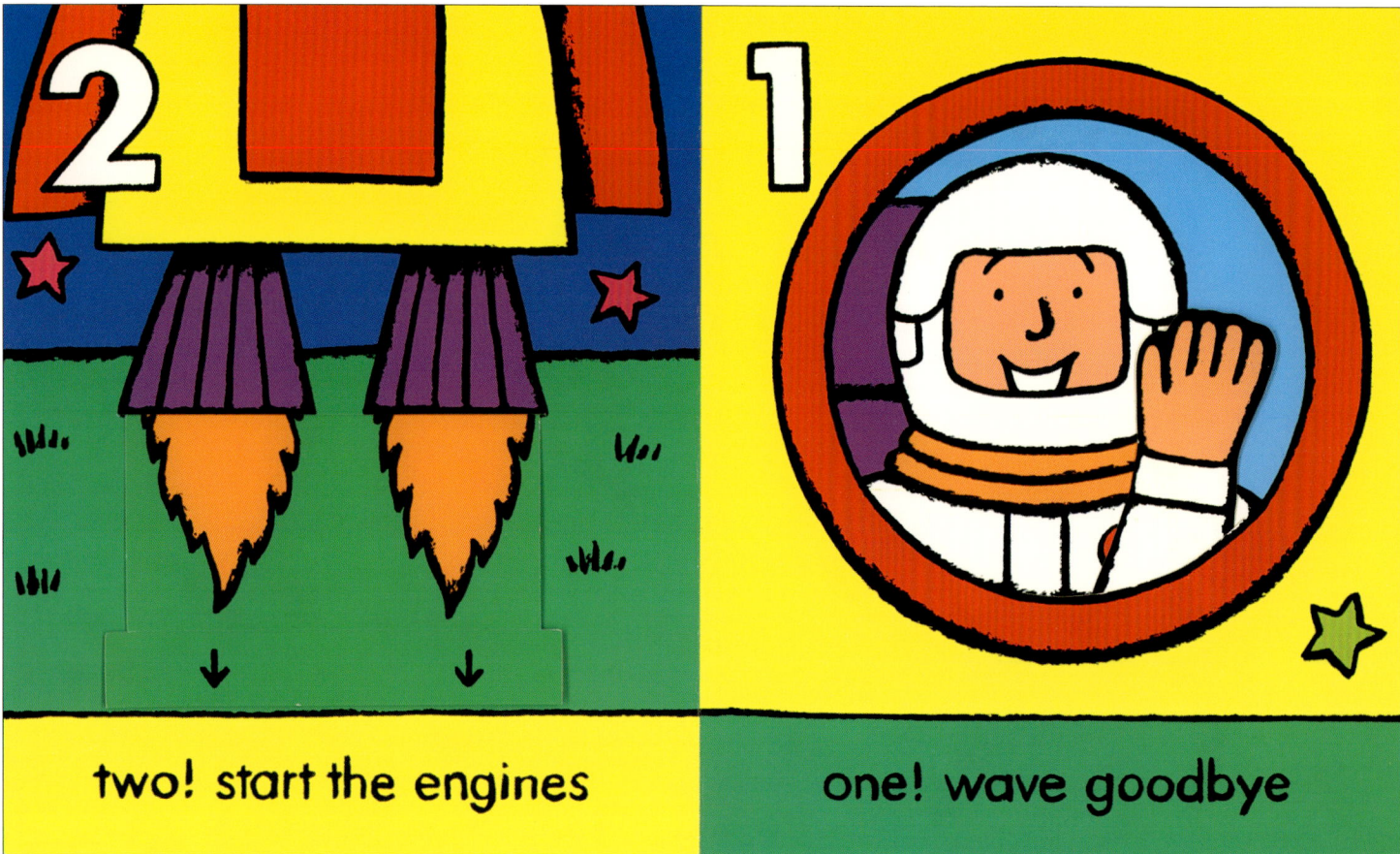

two! start the engines

one! wave goodbye

It was expensive because I was paying for John's time. But now, what I do is I photocopy everything up and I draw up very detailed sheets with all the colours. For the first time there's no speculation about the colours. At first it was crazy, we were making up the colours on the screen. Now I have a Pantone booklet and I mark up absolutely everything to make sure that there's no area of doubt for John. I'd never thought that colouring on a computer could actually be that personal, that people colour in different ways on a computer, it's unbelievable.

Well in terms of things you take for granted, I just took it for granted that someone would know where the sky's going to go. It's just little patches here and there and I just completely automatically know where the sky background will go but somebody else won't realise that that was more, that triangular shape there should be sky and it's very difficult to keep your eye on everything. Now I draw up a very, very detailed sheet and for example I think I've put hundreds and hundreds of NBs. You discover that at the crucial stage it's impossible to tell on a computer. He's got quite a big screen but even so you just can't train yourself to robotically scan across it. If I had the time I suppose I should train to do it all myself, but I'm too busy and I'd never get to the stage that John's at. He does it very quickly and he's been doing it for years and years.

We have worked out a good system and the last thing I did with him I was really pleased with. It was quite complicated, and had very detailed pictures with lots of characters and overlapping textures. We have worked out a very good communication system now, and he understands my notes. But I leave nothing to chance at all. When I started on computers I thought

it's going to be so easy, it's going to be fantastic. I never realised that the computer was going to create so many problems. For example the cheeks on the boy's face. If I was doing it as actual artwork it will take thirty seconds, with a red pencil and a cotton bud, and I'd have the cheek. On a computer you've got to position the thing, you've got to come up with some technique that will replicate my normal method.

Inside spread from *Rocket Countdown.*

An example of a plan prepared for a computer illustration.

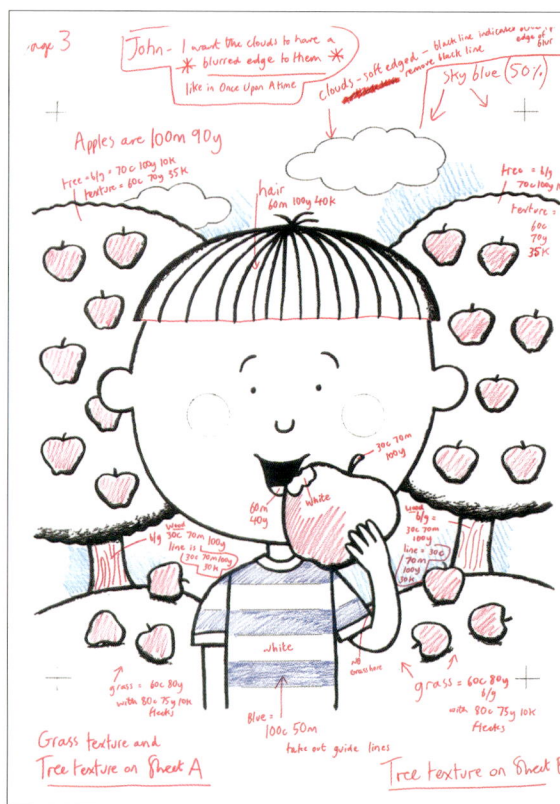

THE TIME IT TOOK TOM

Nick Sharratt   Stephen Tucker

Cover, spread and endpiece for
The Time it Took Tom, Stephen Tucker
and Nick Sharratt, published by
Scholastic Children's Books,
London, 1998.

I've just done a really nice project with John. It's a book with lots and lots of texture and patterns devised by me. These textures and patterns are everywhere, and we did this much more efficiently and quickly than earlier projects. I have my charcoal drawing scanned in as line. In the early days this did prove problematic,

because I didn't know the line breaks up and the little holes within the line needed to have colour behind them and things that I never envisaged, and then I'd make up fairly simple patterns that are all, almost always line. You can have a lot of fun playing around with them, and I like the effect. I just love bright colours and so do the children. I actually do use quite a lot of this pure magenta when I can, the brighter the better really, I have been through lots of processes searching for the Holy Grail of perfectly flat colour. I've used animation, paints and various washes but the computer is fantastic for really flat colour and I now have a list of colours I know are going to work, like a certain red. I have a palette of colours which are locked into the system, and these are the colours I like to work with.

We've got a green, it's called (they've all got names from books) 'the time it took Tom' green which is a lime green. This is such a difficult colour to reproduce, if you did full colour artwork you're not guaranteed a good reproduction. It could be murky. This is a computer green which I like to work with.

Sometimes I think it would be easier to draw a repeat wallpaper pattern than trying to drop the damn thing in. With *The Time it Took Tom*, the brief was to do a book about Time. The writer and I came up with this

Look what I've found, all wriggly and pink, right here on the ground. What do you think? YUK!

Spread from *My Days Out*, Stephen Tucker and Nick Sharratt, published by Oxford University Press, 1999.

story about a boy who paints everything red, but I think partly that was made possible by the fact that I knew I could get a fantastic flat red. The boy completely obliterates a living room in a coat of flat red paint, and I really liked the idea of a detailed patterned living room contrasted with this huge area of flat red, and I knew that I could do that on a computer far more effectively than a conventional painted method.

This actually happened, I was at primary school with a boy that did it. He painted the wood panelling in his living room a green colour. I can't imagine how I would have tried to do this if I hadn't done it on the computer. Did you spot the very, very end? The cat appears in blue!

Because the story is all about time I wanted to indicate the passage of time When we get towards the end of the story and there's a very long sort of poem with lots and lots of tiny little images taken from the bigger drawings at the beginning. You can very easily play with the scale, and I think I drew all the pictures at the same scale that I drew the original room, and then on the computer they were just shrunk down to get smaller and smaller and smaller as the time passed.

I had a lot of fun doing this book. As soon as you hand the book in you always forget about all the work that went into it, but I know this book went back and forth and back and forth at every stage and I think it went through two or three sets of proofs to get the colours just right, so it was extremely hard work.

I have done 50 or so picture books for children, I don't exclusively use computers. I do books with watercolour I use charcoal and then I fix it and then I colour it in with liquid acrylic inks, but it's a different feel. In a way once you've conquered the technical process of finding out how to make the computer do something, you can be reasonably sure that that can be pushed further in time. Each time we do a little bit more, like in this one, they may be only very small things. But they add up.

I did a split page book cut into two which gives you 121 combinations. I've done a split page book cut into three, this is just with 12 spreads, allowing for pages that are stuck down at the beginning and the end, and with three splits you get 2666 different combinations, and with this one, which is cut into four, you get 14,500 different combinations. So from an editorial point of view it's a bit of a trial. You put together a dummy and you think you've worked out all the text (this is quite a texty story), and then you discover that you've got some combination which doesn't flow properly. It took ages, it really took ages to get it all to flow. At first it seemed like a really simple idea.

Teachers have told me the split books are good for reluctant readers because you don't have to start at the beginning and go to the end, you can turn the page in any way that you want and once you know the format of the book like with *Ketchup on Your Cornflakes*, anybody can read it to themselves. It always starts 'Do you like?' and then you just see the picture clues and you know you can read it. I do take dummies into classrooms to test them out and it's really useful, you can pick up things that the children relate to and what they don't.

Most publishers have a publicity department and they have a pool of authors who go to schools, and schools call up and say have you got an author, or they request that you go and see them, and I'm happy to do that, I've cut back now because I'm really busy. But it's great and I have actually have had some ideas directly from contact with children. *Rocket Countdown* is actually dedicated to a little boy, who came and saw me with his own little rocket book. I adapted his idea and turned it into this one. So that was absolutely direct inspiration.

A Shark in the Park is a book that I've done, it came about partly because it seems that everybody now wants to be a marine biologist at school, it's like the number one job that they want to do. I don't know where it's come from but you go into a school and I say 'I always wanted to be an illustrator' and does anybody know what they want to be, and almost without fail somebody will say they want to be a marine biologist. So I know that Oceanography is quite a good subject and I think they all know their sharks and their sea-life. Dinosaurs are another one that they absolutely know about, and I've done a dinosaur book or two, you can pick up lots of information going round to schools.

I usually get about 4–6 months from commission I suppose, but I've always kind of got so much work on that it's always down to the last month, I always I keep to my deadlines though!

I used to get up at 6 or 7, working seven days a week, but now I start at 9 and I work till half 6 or 7, office hours really. I've just about gotten over thinking this might be my last job and if I say no it definitely will be. I'm much better at taking on less work. I have some really nice projects now, they're ones that I really want to do and not the ones that I've just said yes to because of the need to say yes to everything.

Spreads from *Buzz Buzz, Bumble Jelly,* **published by Scholastic Children's Books, London, 2000.**

Yippee!
A wibbly, wobbly

cowboy

Whirrrr!
A heli-

bee

John Lawrence

Speaking to Martin Salisbury

I have been fortunate to count John Lawrence as a friend for some years now, since he and his wife Myra moved from London to Cambridge, Myra's family home, and I began to pester him to come and talk about his work to the APU Cambridge Illustration students. This he kindly did, and is now looking forward to teaching students on the new MA in Children's Book Illustration.

It doesn't seem possible that John's work has now been published across six decades – his work first appeared in print in the late nineteen fifties. This is a man who regularly cycles and goes running through the nearby woods.

Over the last year or so, when we have chatted over a pint after the weekly life-drawing class and we have exchanged updates about our respective current commissions, I have been hearing about the progress of a picture-book that John has illustrated for Walker Books. Despite a lifetime of achievement in the world of illustration John Lawrence is an extraordinarily modest man, an inveterate worrier, sometimes seeming to be riddled with insecurity about his work. Nevertheless, I had been able to tell that this new book was something special and this was borne out as I turned up at his studio for a chat. The newly arrived printouts of the spreads for This Little Chick[1] were laid out on the floor and he was casting a critical eye over them for any last-minute changes. It was now clear why John had taken time out from all other commissions to concentrate on this. The words 'traditional' and 'English' tend to be used in connection with his work. To me, this new picture book exhibits all that is good about those qualities while also appearing somehow incredibly contemporary and universal. There is the evidence of the well-known feel for the chapbook tradition and the familiar vinyl engraving technique, and yet there are new experiments with textured backgrounds and flat colours. These, it transpires, have been produced separately and put together by the designer. He is clearly excited about this book and with good reason.

With these page printouts still laid across the floor of the studio, amongst the piles of books, the presses and other paraphernalia of a busy studio, we settled down to look back over a long, but still growing, career. I asked whether he had always drawn as a child.

'I'd always drawn, yes, but there was hardly any art teaching at the school that I went to. So all of my drawing was in the form of cartoons really, which is how so many people start out. I'd spend hours and hours pouring over Walt Disney images and copying them and everything. I was fascinated by things like the way Donald Duck's beak would curve up at the end, and I suppose I was teaching myself to draw really. And of course the comedy side of it interested me as well.'

He then went to art school in Hastings, the town where he was brought up. 'I think it was actually quite a good place to go. The principle was Vincent Lines, a sensitive and able watercolourist, very traditional. He had been a great friend of Thomas Hennell, and they had both been taught by A. S. Hartrick a brilliant lithographer and fine draughtsman.

'So it was through Vincent Lines that I learned about Hennell.' At this point I was shown a project on Hennell that John had done later while a student at the Central. 'I found it the other day – extraordinary. This is how things were done in those days – look.' The project involved an essay about the work of Thomas Hennell accompanied by John's meticulous copies of his drawings – virtually indistinguishable from the originals.

'Anyway, I'm just showing you that because it shows the sort of influences which were at work at that time. But in those early days we were drawing the whole time. I mean we had costume, life, anatomy. And then we had a bit of architecture. We had painting – it was called composition actually. Printmaking, lithography – the whole week – it was a fantastic background, actually.'

'But I was very ambitious to go to one of the London art schools. For one thing, I wanted to get out of my home town, find some freedom! But I didn't have any money and my parents couldn't help much. And I couldn't get a grant because they'd say, "Why are we giving you a grant to go to London when you could do

1. *This Little Chick*, illustrated by John Lawrence, Walker Books, not yet published.

All Afloat : Coat

From *Rabbit and Pork, Rhyming Talk*, Hamish Hamilton/Crowell, 1975.

the course here?" So I thought, "Well, I've got to do my National Service at some point, so I might as well do it now and see what happens." And so I managed to get a commission – a bit of luck really. I was paid as a captain out in West Africa, they were very short-staffed and many of us were working in positions higher than our own ranks really. And there wasn't much to spend money on apart from beer, which we drank a lot of, but it was cheap, and so I came out of the army with a fair amount saved up. So I immediately set out to get into one of the London art schools. I applied to Goldsmiths' and then an old friend of mine, Philip Thompson, the Graphic Artist, who had preceded me at Hastings (we all thought he was God), told me, "You don't want to go there, you should go to the Central to do illustration."

'So anyway, I was offered a place at Goldsmiths' and I cancelled it. I mean I can't believe it, looking back now. You wouldn't do that sort of thing nowadays, would you? And I turned up at the Central with my portfolio for interview and I thought, 'My God, what have I done?' – the whole thing was dawning on me. But I think the fact that I had a lot of drawings from my time in West Africa helped me to stand out a bit. So I got in, luckily.'

At the Central he studied under people such as Keith Vaughan and Gertrude Hermes.

'We had Keith Vaughan for illustration. He really taught in terms of black and white illustration of course. He would bring in the Argosy magazine, which is a magazine of short stories, and he would just hand them out. And he would bring in sheets of stuff cut out from the *Radio Times* – particularly John Minton's work. And he'd come round and talk to you I suppose about tone and composition which was really quite good. It was the old NDD idea of composition but you wouldn't talk in terms of composition as "a subject" these days. Also, illustration wasn't really taught in terms of the interpretation of text or the storytelling side. It was more a case of – you'd have a drawing and it was about how to make it into a better drawing. Keith Vaughan was a bit of a 'one off' anyway, but this was still the fifties and people were teaching 'art' rather than applied art. And of course he hadn't been to art school, he went to an advertising agency at the age of sixteen.'

I mentioned that many of the artists whose illustrative work was so influential at this time had trained as painters.

'Yes, that's right, and of course people like Ravilious and Bawden were taught by Paul Nash who wasn't teaching "illustration", was he? They all say they owe a great debt to him. Actually, in those days these people were known as "painter illustrators", which I

Spread from *This Little Chick*.

think nowadays would be regarded as an insult. So anyway, we had life drawing all day Monday with William Roberts. We had Mervyn Peake and Maurice Kestelman. William Roberts was quite an elderly man then and Mervyn Peake had done all that brilliant work but he wasn't the well-known artist that he became after his death. He'd done wonderful things like *Captain Slaughterboard* and so on but the children's book market hadn't really opened up in any big way, you know. In fact they were really only seen by privileged middle-class people.'

Did he know at this time that illustration was the area that he wanted to work within?

'Yes, I think so. I always wanted to be either a journalist or a cartoonist. I wanted to be involved with books, with narrative. I always loved literature, I read a lot.'

Another tutor mentioned was Lawrence Scarfe.

I had not known that John had been taught by him, so a long conversation followed about his work, both of us agreeing that the man best known for his work on *The Saturday Book* should be much more widely known and appreciated. John feels that in many ways he learned more from Scarfe about drawing – the freedom of drawing – than from Vaughan, who was more concerned with design, and the distribution of blacks and whites.

'Then on Thursdays we had wood engraving with Gert Hermes and on Fridays lithography with Clarke Hutton.'

A similar conversation ensues about the work of Hutton, another largely forgotten artist.

'But I suppose the people we were all most influenced by were Minton, Vaughan, Anthony Gross, Bawden and Ardizzone.'

John Lawrence left the Central some time after

2. *Black's Children's Encyclopaedia*, W. Worthy and R. J. Unstead, A & C Black, 1961.

Colin Forbes had taken over as Head of Department. "He had a lot of contacts and we would all go and ask him and get a list of people to see. This was mainly in the design areas, but you would look up publishing in *The Bookseller* which even then had all those adverts at the back. And so I took my portfolio around and eventually the first real job came. I went to an agent called "Saxon Artists" who were representing all sorts of people including Fritz Wegner – a good friend of mine now – and they said they liked my work but they had enough of that sort of thing. But they gave me the name of a man called William Worthy who was in the process of putting together a children's encyclopaedia[2] and was looking for an artist. He was a schoolmaster. I did two volumes of that.'

We spent some time looking at copies of these volumes – profusely illustrated and attractively designed with a strong 1950s feel. 'You'll see all my influences very clearly in there! But it was fantastic to get the work. It kept us going financially for months and I really learned my craft dong that. I had to work very small, which I hadn't done before. They used the lino-cut designs on the jacket which was really quite brave of them. So I did all sorts of jobs over a period of years and then I had a bit of a breakthrough because through Gert Hermes I got a job for Benson's, I did a full page and that went in all the magazines, so that was a good point of reference for people, they were more confident about employing you if you'd been published. I was taking anything I could get then – book jackets and things, often poorly paid, just because we needed to survive.'

Knowing that John has taught in art schools for many years, I asked when he gained his first part-time teaching position. 'There again, I was lucky, because when I left the Central Colin Forbes said to me,

This little chick from over the way went to laze with the cows one day.

"William Stobbs is at Maidstone, and I think he's looking for some people to do some teaching." And I got a job at Maidstone for a day a week. And that's what kept us, really. And I was there for two years and ... I'm sure I've told you this story, Martin, but I was all into the German Expressionists at the time, and I had all the students doing big lino cuts. William Stobbs came in one day and took me aside and said, "Well, John, this isn't really what we want you to be doing. Perhaps you could take them out drawing." Of course he was into all this clean Swiss graphics. This was after I had been there two years, and it was the first time he'd found me. Well, I thought, "Blow that!" I needed the money, but ... Anyway, then Gert Hermes recommended me to go to Camberwell to take over from Frank Martin. And I got the job there, and John Biggs asked me to go to Brighton to teach wood-engraving, so after giving up in a cavalier fashion my day's teaching at Maidstone I found myself with two days' teaching. So that was

riches indeed. After a while I gave up Brighton and just kept Camberwell and I was there until '94.'

'The next milestone work-wise was my first introduction to the Folio Society in '67 or '68 and I did *Colonel Jack*[3] and then *Diary of a Nobody*[4], *Tristram Shandy*[5] and all sorts of other books. And so I felt then that I was sort of plugged in to real narrative illustration. And it just went on from there.'

'Then in 1968 I went to see Hamish Hamilton. I'd been trawling this book around for ages called *The Giant of Grabbist*.[6] Looking at it now – look at this, this is the early days of colour printing, really – it's bumped up to the nines and out of register. Anyway, Michael Brown there said that Julia McRae was really interested in it. I was working then much more with guache, heavy colours and things and was still using the pen, and of course it would all get sort of clogged up! So it's not entirely happy, but I'm still quite fond of it. All done with fountain pen, actually. So that was my first

Spread from *This Little Chick*.

3. *Colonel Jack*, Daniel Defoe, Folio, 196
4. *The Diary of a Nobody*, George and Weedon Grossmith, Folio, 1969.
5. *The Life and Opinions of Tristram Shand Gentleman*, Laurence Sterne, Folio, 1970

6. *The Giant of Grabbist*, John Lawrence, Hamish Hamilton, 1968.

And what do you think they heard him say?

7. *Pope Leo's Elephant*, John Lawrence, Hamish Hamilton, 1969.

picture-book. I found the story in a Kathleen Briggs collection of folk tales. I've never been able to come up with very original story lines so I just embroidered it a little and Julia or one of the other editors actually put it into proper English. I did two others for them fairly quickly afterwards including *Pope Leo's Elephant*.[7] And that actually did rather well for a time. Again, I found the story. I used to do little black and white drawings for *The Tablet*, the Roman Catholic magazine, and I found this story about a pope who had been given an elephant. This was in the time of Raphael, and I thought this would be a marvellous story. Julia seemed to like it, and of course it was set in Italy which was lovely to do.'

As we looked through the book John became very excited about how the elephant helped to build St Peter's '…and there was a fire and he put the fire out, you see… and then, of course, he was a great hero!' John seemed to have temporarily forgotten the fact that it was he who had created this lovely book. We couldn't help but laugh

at the print quality – the colour and poor registration. 'Don't look at it too long or your eyes will go!'

The nineteen seventies became an increasingly prolific time for him, with a great deal of work for the Folio Society and Hamish Hamilton. John pulled down several of these from the bookcase as examples, always worrying that 'some are better than others … I expect as a haunter of second-hand book shops, Martin, you have unearthed all my sins.'

'But with Hamish Hamilton I was lucky in being able to work with some marvellous writers such as E. Nesbit and Janet McNeill.'

He thinks of himself primarily as a book illustrator now. 'I've never enjoyed those sort of "one-off" jobs. The truth is, I go to pieces under pressure. Some people seem to thrive on it. But, as you know, with books, although you've got a schedule you are doing lots of drawings, all related to one another, and that's my safety net really.'

Speaking more specifically about children's books he feels that the idea of working for 'the child in one's self' is exactly right. 'Yes, I'm entirely in agreement with that.' He feels sad, though, that some of the books of which he is most proud have received excellent reviews but have not sold well, perhaps because they are too 'arty'. It is particularly true, he says, of the *New Treasury of Poetry*.[8] 'That book is actually one of the few books that I am actually quite proud of. It's a 'look-into' book, really. I mean there's nothing more thrilling than finding a really old, battered copy of anything I've done because you think, "God, someone's really been looking at this!" There are certain artists who can make beautiful books but which also have mass appeal – Quentin Blake for example. One can only do one's very best and I suppose history will judge.'

John Lawrence has worked across a wide range of book genres and I asked him about some of the more location- or 'reportage'-based projects such as the *Cranks* healthfood books[9] and Richard Adams' *Nature Diary*.[10] 'Yes, I enjoyed those immensely. I mean in an ideal world, you know, you'd get at least one of those jobs every two years or something, so that you could have a month or two just doing what we all ought to be doing more of anyway, which is going out and drawing in the sketchbook. I know you like to use sketchbooks. I do when I'm travelling, but when you're at home

Top: **Red sketchbook (Portugal)**.
Above & left: **from Entertaining with Cranks.**
Facing page: **from A New Treasury of Poetry.**

8. *A New Treasury of Poetry*, selected and introduced by Neil Philip, Blackie, 1990.

9. *The Cranks Recipe Book*, David and Kay Canter and Daphne Swann, Dent, 1982, and *Entertaining with Cranks*, Dent, 1985.

10. *A Nature Diary*, Richard Adams, Viking, 1985.

you're always worrying about the next job and the mind isn't free enough. So it's nice when you actually get a job which involves going out and drawing on location.'

We spoke a little about the idea of exhibiting work – taking time out to produce a set of prints for example, and it was clear that this is not high on the agenda – in fact it brought us back to the new picture-book – in itself a set of prints. 'Well, you are making your own art with this, really, in a way. I wanted to get everything

exactly right with this. For example the sense of the haze of a summer's day behind the cow in the meadow – I needed to get that colour exactly right. So it boils down in the end to doing what you want to do.'

The idea of retirement horrifies him. 'No, I couldn't do that, oh no. I wouldn't know what to do … no. Giving up my agent I regarded as a sort of retirement from a certain kind of work that I no longer wanted to do. I used to get so anxious about those urgent phone calls. Another thing is, I'm not sure that editors and so on realise the commitment we have to our work. At one time you would always be sent proofs and things. Now it's much more casual. You send off work and you're biting your fingernails for days and you won't phone them because you think, "If I phone them there's bound to be something wrong", but you don't hear anything and then you finally learn that everything was fine.'

Does he feel that today's illustration graduates have a chance of a long career such as his? 'Apart from anything else, Martin, the times might not allow that, the changing markets and everything. I mean, one hopes that books will go on for ever, but the changing media and everything – well, we just don't know, do we? I suppose it's a sort of cliche, but I do believe that if someone can actually draw – it's through drawing that you find your individuality really.'

Facing page and below: **from White Sketchbook (Italy).** *Bottom:* **from Red Sketchbook (Portugal).**

An afternoon with **Susan Einzig**

Martin Salisbury

Susan Einzig came to England at the age of sixteen as a German Jewish refugee, shortly before the outbreak of the Second World War. In the years immediately after the war she was very much a part of the heady spiral of creativity that was the so-called Soho scene – the Jazz Years, a period when the nation's appetite for art, literature and music seemed insatiable after the years of deprivation and austerity. The spirit of 'Neo Romanticism' flowered and took hold for a few short years.

As an illustrator, Ms Einzig produced drawings regularly for publications such as *Radio Times*, *Lilliput*, and *Our Time*, and went on to illustrate a number of books, including one of the most important twentieth-century children's books, *Tom's Midnight Garden* by Philippa Pearce.[1] Her work as a painter, illustrator and teacher (she taught illustration at Chelsea School of Art for many years) is greatly admired by her peers. When I asked her whether or not she still paints, she answered. 'Of course... it's all I do!'

This was very much confirmed as I called on her at her home/studio in a quiet West London street on a late summer afternoon.

I asked her first whether she had known as a child in Germany that she wanted to be an artist.

1. Oxford, 1958.

Facing page: **dust-jacket Tom's Midnight Garden.**
Below: **park landscape, watercolour, 20″ × 25″.**

Tom's Midnight Garden

Philippa Pearce

[SE] Always, yes, though I think what might have happened if the Nazis hadn't come, is that I might have gone into the theatre or become a writer. But these are only conjectures. As Lucien Freud says, 'we're here because we're here because we're here'.

My father wanted me to be an artist – at least his idea was that I should do fashion drawings for the rag trade. Well, it turned out that I was utterly unsuited to doing that. I am hopelessly uncommercial. Instead I drew and drew – I was really serious about that. I also discovered that I could draw out of my head, which was very exciting, and I started to illustrate stories I was reading, which happened to be Oscar Wilde's fairy stories. I have always lived in imaginative literature, which somehow seemed more real to me, more about what experience really feels like, than what is called reality. Proust said that the only real life is the life of literature – I am not unsympathetic to that idea.

When I came to England in the spring of 1939, just three months before war broke out, I enrolled as a student at the Central School of Arts and Crafts. I was taught drawing by Bernard Mekinsky, William Roberts and Maurice Kestelman, illustration by John Farleigh and wood engraving by Gertrude Hermes. It was the tail end of the Arts and Crafts movement, and the emphasis was very much on form and craft. This has all changed of course, it's another world now. Then, I spent most of my time life drawing, and the rest printmaking and illustrating books. I was the youngest student there, and I worked hard and was horribly good and conscientious and tried to fit in, which I patently didn't. I spoke very little English and was more than a little lost in what was a totally different culture to the one I'd grown up in.

And the London Art Schools were all moved to Northampton for the duration of the war, weren't they?
Yes. We all spent the first six months of the war waiting for the air raids to start, and I remember spending hours in the basement of the Central rolling bandages in readiness for the anticipated carnage, which in the event didn't materialise, at least not until months later. When the bombs started to drop, the London Art Schools were closed and were moved to Northampton. There weren't many of us left – most staff and students had been called up, so it was quite a small and tight little group that formed its own world in Northampton, until then known only for the manufacture of shoes and bicycles. The result for me was that I got to know people I would never have met had we stayed in London, and I became a part of a cultural environment that was far more sophisticated and idealistic than the utilitarian training for commercial art that would have been mine except for the war. In fact, Northampton was artistically rather an interesting place. The local vicar was an enthusiastic collector of avant-garde art, and thanks to him has a beautiful Henry Moore sculpture in the local church. Like many towns all over the country there was a much loved and thriving repertory theatre, all red plush and gilded mouldings, and a small group of us became involved in painting

From *Tom's Midnight Garden*.

the weekly scenery which was not only great training, but wonderful fun. One of our teachers was the painter, Bernard Adeney, who with his artist wife, Noël, and son, Richard and daughter Charlotte, rented a large Victorian house for the duration and I became a close friend of theirs – they sort of adopted me as a third child. Bernard and Noël were part of Bloomsbury, and close friends of Vanessa Bell, Duncan Grant and Dora Carrington. Their house was full of exquisite old furniture and paintings. Noël cooked delicious meals, full of garlic and aromatic herbs, which they grew in their back garden. Richard was a flautist with the newly formed London Philharmonic Orchestra and Charlotte, who was a painting student and became my great friend, played the cello. We tried to play trios, but I'm afraid my piano playing wasn't really up to it. It was through them that I discovered painting. There were also a number of distinguished art historians, who came down from London and gave slide lectures – I particularly remember one about Constable's skies – I have never forgotten the feeling of excitement I felt at the revelation that one could look at clouds and sky and dream and make painting like that. It was all very escapist from what was going on out there, people fighting the war and getting killed. My parents, from whom I no longer had any news, were trapped in Berlin, and I didn't know whether they were still alive. I later heard that my father had been deported and died in a concentration camp. It was at this time, through reading and my own feelings of isolation and conflict, that I became politicised. It became quite obvious to me that socialism was the only sane answer to a mad and barbaric world.

You worked in factories during the war, I gather?

Yes, that was pretty grim. I was completely separated from everything that mattered to me, and the work was repetitive and soul destroying. It was slavery. I also managed to get the sack from each and every job – quite an achievement during wartime. Towards the end of the war I met Noël Carrington who ran a publishing firm, Transatlantic Arts.

2. Transatlantic Arts, 1946.

3. *Alphabet and Image*, a quarterly journal of the visual arts published by The Shenval Press in the 1940s.

Illustration for *The Tragedy of Nan*, *The Radio Times*, 13.6.58.

And you worked with him on *Mary Belinda and the Ten Aunts*.[2]

Yes. I enjoyed that. The text was charming, and I had to do all the illustrations in six-colour hand lithography on zinc plates. When the finished work went to the printers, Cowells of Ipswich, I was put into their special artist's room, and worked on the proofs with one of their marvellous technicians. I might say 'Oh, this yellow is a bit too orange', and he would take it away and come back, and it would be just right. A real collaboration.

It's not quite like that now.

When the war was over, I started to freelance. The first person who gave me work was Robert Harling, who published *Alphabet and Image*.[3] I was terribly nervous and inexperienced, but he was very supportive, and somehow I managed with great difficulty to produce the work, and got paid too.

There was quite a lot of interesting work about. There were many refugees from Central Europe, who had been book and magazine publishers in Germany, France and Austria, and who brought with them their culture of producing beautiful, illustrated books. It was before television and dumbing down. There was a great upsurge of creativity, and painters were commissioned to illustrate books, design book jackets and work for advertising. As for me, I had to get the freelance jobs – I had to pay the rent. I hadn't really been trained, but I just had to cope and I learned on the job.

Were you hawking your portfolio around?

Oh, forever. And then, after a bit, I thought I'd better get a 'proper' job, and I went to see William Johnson at Camberwell, who had taught me at Northampton, and he gave me a couple of days a week teaching juniors. At that time they used to put kids of fourteen or even younger into Art Schools, if they weren't particularly academic, and it was thought that they might perhaps be artistic. I was about twenty-one or two, and hardly able to cope with my own work or life, and trying to teach and control a large class of stroppy adolescents, a lot of whom didn't understand what they were doing in this funny place, wasn't exactly my cup of tea. Still, there were some bright exceptions, and I had Euan Uglow and Terry Scales amongst my students and they made up for all the rest. I also got to teach ex-servicemen, who had been given government grants to retrain – one of whom was Humphrey Littleton and the other Wally Fawkes, the jazz clarinettist and cartoonist.

And then I met John Minton and Keith Vaughan who were teaching painting and illustration at Camberwell. Johnny was the most charismatic and brilliant teacher, the centre of an adoring group of students, over whom he had great influence. I was quickly drawn into this group, and began to share a lot of my teaching time with Johnny. We all used to meet at weekends and draw each other, we went to the cinema and discovered the films of Jean Renoir, René Clair and Marcel Carné; we went to the theatre and discovered Tennessee Williams, we heard Peter Pears sing Peter Grimes and Billy Budd, and we jived and jitter bugged to Humphrey Littleton's jazzband every Monday evening. We also got sucked into the drinking scene in Soho. It was all over within two or three years, but in my memory it seems to have been much longer. We lived so intensely, and so much experience was crammed into such a comparatively short period; and we were young and time seemed to go on forever. I suppose some of my most profound influences stem from these years.

Susan Einzig

These artists, Minton, yourself, Colquhoun, MacBride and Keith Vaughan have subsequently been grouped together as the Neo-Romantic movement. Do you think the term is meaningful – was it thought of in those terms at the time?

Not really. Like most labels it's very reductionist. The Roberts came from the school of Paris, from Picasso, Johnny from a mixture of Picasso, Samuel Palmer and contemporary cinema, and Keith from Picasso, Cézanne and painters like Graham Sutherland. My own background was even more complicated.

The word 'facility' is often used in relation to John Minton's work, but you have said that you have always found drawing hard work.[4]

Yes, for me work has never come easily. I am never satisfied with anything I do, and I am forever changing everything, until someone comes and takes it away.

When I was doing my freelance illustrations, I used to pile on white paint, and cut and patch the paper until the drawings ended up like three-dimensional reliefs. It was a wonder they got reproduced at all.

There is a wonderful Minton drawing, one of my favourites, on the cover of the magazine *Our Time*, about 1947. Do you know it? It's a scene of wild dancing in a jazz club with Minton himself in the foreground.

I must have seen it at the time, but I don't remember it – I used to work for *Our Time* as well when John Mortimer was involved with it.

As well as your work for magazines, you are also, of course, known as a book illustrator, and perhaps best of all for that marvellous book *Tom's Midnight Garden* by Philippa Pearce. I think of that as one of those rare

John Minton: cover illustration for *Our Time* magazine 1947.

4. Interview with David Driver, The Art of Radio Times. BBC/European Illustration 1981.

examples of excellent writing and excellent illustration meeting in harmony. How did that come about?

I had been to see the children's book editor at Oxford University Press, who had looked at my work and seemed very unsure about it. However, she gave me Philippa Pearce's manuscript to try and see if I could do it. I did two or three drawings and took them to show her, and she then asked me to do the book. She was rather surprised at the way it all turned out. It is astonishing that I was paid just £100 for the whole thing.

There is a strong sense of place in your drawings. I understand that you visited Cambridge where Philippa Pearce lived, and still lives, to research the work. I have always been convinced that the little iron bridge in one of the drawings is based on one I know in Cambridge.

Well no, that bridge was on the canal in Camberwell, where Johnny and I used to go for walks after we finished

From *Tom's Midnight Garden*.

From *The Story of John Keats*, by
Robert Gittings and Jo Manton,
Methuen, 1962.

teaching. My pictures have always been based upon memories of real experiences or remembered images from films or imagined scenes from literature. I would also draw objects from my house and other places.

At this point in the interview we decided to adjourn to Ms Einzig's studio to look at the work she is doing now. Having spoken of her tendency to 'live in the past' in terms of literature and society generally, the opposite is clearly the case with her own painting now. The studio was alive with current work – paintings, drawings, prints; work-in-progress on the wall, a large

painting showing two ethereal figures merging into a wooded scene. A magical, lyrical painting. Talking about her current work she becomes even more alive and animated.

Susan Einzig's passion for painting, drawing and literature, and the evidence of this in her illustrative work, is perhaps the key to the reason why, despite a comparatively small output in terms of illustrated books, she is one of the most important and respected graphic artists of her generation.

I am grateful to Ms Einzig for allowing me into her home for an enchanting afternoon.

Girl reading by a window,
etching 15″× 17″.

Zennor, etching 20″× 21″.

Figures in a park,
oil on canvas 25″× 31″.

Bishop's park,
oil on canvas
26″× 34″.

SUSAN EINZIG

A lunch with Fritz Wegner

Tom Morgan-Jones

I was aged seven when I first saw a copy of *Fattypuffs & Thinifers*. It was lying among hundreds of other books on a school desk, but it was by far the best looking book there. It had a witty, funny, spiky, and strangely gracious drawing of two soldiers on the front, along with its beautifully rendered title, *Fattypuffs & Thinifers*. I had fallen in love with a book. Perhaps sometimes you should judge a book by its cover. It was Book Club day. I looked to my hands where I counted my owl tokens, and then I counted the coins in my pocket. It would take me two weeks to save enough money to buy the book. So the book Club people kept it for me, in a cardboard box with my name written on a piece of paper, put inside. At last, when I did buy the book I think it changed my life.

I loved that book, and later when I was in my twenties I wanted to find it, and couldn't. I looked everywhere, all through the book shelves at my parents house, and all through their loft. I looked through all their boxes. I looked in lots of book shops. I asked for it in lots of book shops, only to hear 'Oh yes I remember that, it was wonderful, but I don't think you'll be able to get hold of a copy now, sorry', and 'Sorry, what did you say? *Fattypuffs & Thinifers*? Would you spell that?' 'Written by André Maurois? Would you spell that?' 'Illustrated by who? Fritz Wegner?' and 'Would you spell that? Oh no, sorry, that is been out of print a long time now.'

Right, pot luck with charity shops and an onslaught of second-hand book shops, and antiquarian book shops is required, I thought. That pleasure kept me busy for a long time, until one day, at one of the Russell Square book fairs, my arm shot out and there was this big beautiful hardback book, and all the pictures were there as I remembered them. At last! I had found he chance to be taken on this adventure again, and it made me very happy. 'Oh, you like that book, do you?' said my friend. 'This is a fabulous book, I've been looking for this book for years.' 'Well, in that case Tom, would you like to meet the illustrator? Fritz is a good friend of mine.' Is he? Would I? Could I? Please! Holding my new book I smiled, a very big smile.

I've always remembered Fritz's drawings from *Fattypuffs & Thinifers*, and I've never forgotten the story itself. I think it was possibly the first book I had which gave me a thirst for books. It quite literally opened up a

ANDRÉ MAUROIS

FATTYPUFFS
&
THINIFERS

ILLUSTRATED BY FRITZ WEGNER

THE BODLEY HEAD
LONDON   SYDNEY   TORONTO

Fattypuffs & Thinifers, **written by André Maurois, published by The Bodley Head, London, 1968.**

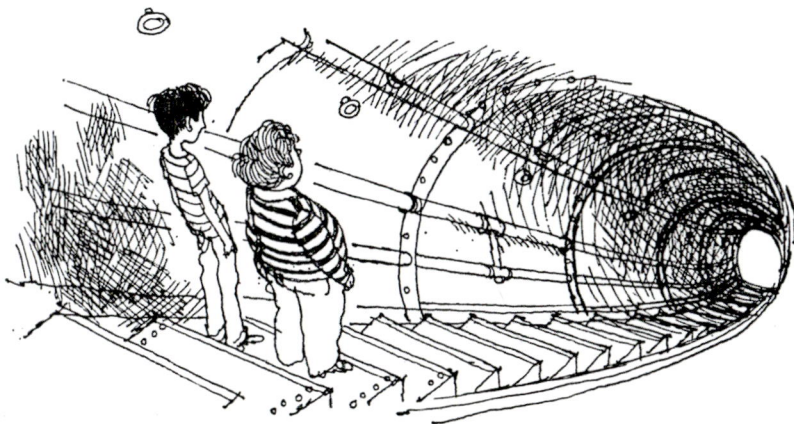

whole new world for me (and you'll find that world between two rocks, down a set of moving stairs…)

I recall the sense of journey, the adventure within the pages, the unfolding story. Both the written word and the illustrations are funny, mischievous, witty and compassionate. That's why I loved it. These days its easier to get hold of a copy. Jane Nissen Books published a new edition in 2000. Fritz has drawn a new illustration for the cover, as well as replacing a handful of the old pictures with new ones which sit alongside all the other classics that are still there, and these days Raymond Briggs is pleased to introduce it. But first, before you pop round the corner to pick up your copy of this beautiful book, to lunch with Mr Wegner…

Fritz, what would you consider to be the most important role of the illustrator?

An illustrator has to enhance the text, and bring an additional dimension to the words. There is no point in repeating laboriously what the word already says. A good illustrator, if he's left to his own devices and his own intentions, can contribute something which makes the story much more interesting.

Fattypuffs & Thinifers was the first book I was offered that gave me that opportunity and I seized it with both arms and hands. I love the story, the humour, and the irony of it, as well. It really appealed to me.

The costumes, or should I say uniforms, are terrific; they are a real celebration of drawing. Did you do much research for those?

I never like labouring from existing studies or reference, I think that one needs to visualise something in a completely uninhibited way. I've trained myself to observe things around me and pretend they're fun so that when I'm given a situation to illustrate I can easily visualise it. The skill comes in putting it down on paper. I do have sketchbooks and studies of things that I've drawn but you can't actually use those specifically for any book illustration; you really have to create a situation that relates to the story. So copying from reference is not a good idea, on the whole.

The practice of drawing from life to hone your skills as a drawer is very important. I think then you draw from that experience. My one regret is that my roughs are very often better than the finished artwork. They're more spontaneous, they have a greater creative sparkle and you don't have to worry too much about sizes and all the constraints you normally have to work with. The rough provides the idea for an illustration and one of the things I admire in Quentin's work is the way he is able to make his finished illustrations look as if they're still those delicious roughs to start with. That's an enviable skill.

Have you picked up any particular skills from someone you can name?

When I first went to St Martin's at the age of 14, one of my teachers was George Mansell, who lectured on lettering and design there at the time. In his own practice he did all sorts of architectural inscriptions, lettering, and manuscript work. Seeing I was a refugee boy, and not particularly well cared for, he invited me to come and live at his home with his French wife, and to assist him in his studio. It was an extremely generous thing to do and indeed I lived with them for several years, learning everything I later knew about lettering, penmanship, gilding and the Roman alphabet. That was the start of an early passion, after which I moved on to doing illustrations. George, an extremely knowledgeable and cultivated man, was able to teach me a great deal more about life. He was responsible for giving me my first formal education in cultural matters, and introducing me to literature, the English language, and a love for the Arts. He had an immense influence on my life and I was very grateful to him. Sadly, of course, he died some time ago, but he bequeathed to me an understanding about typography and lettering: disciplines that have been invaluable to me.

George would have been so pleased to think I ended up teaching illustration at St Martin's, where it all began for me. I remained a visiting member of staff until I retired after 25 years. Perhaps some of my happiest times were spent offering enthusiastic support to students, some of whom became celebrated in their careers, achieving considerable success in different fields of the profession.

What happened after you started freelancing on your own?

I found an agent, Saxon Artists, who represented my work after the war and promoted me more specifically in the advertising field. But I yearned to do book illustration, and finally achieved my first commission

Facing page: Fritz Wegner's Heaven on Earth, **by Fritz Wegner with text by Emma Curzon, published by Walker Books, London, 1992.**

Giant Kippernose and Other Stories, **written by John Cunliffe, published by André Deutsch Limited, London, 1972.**

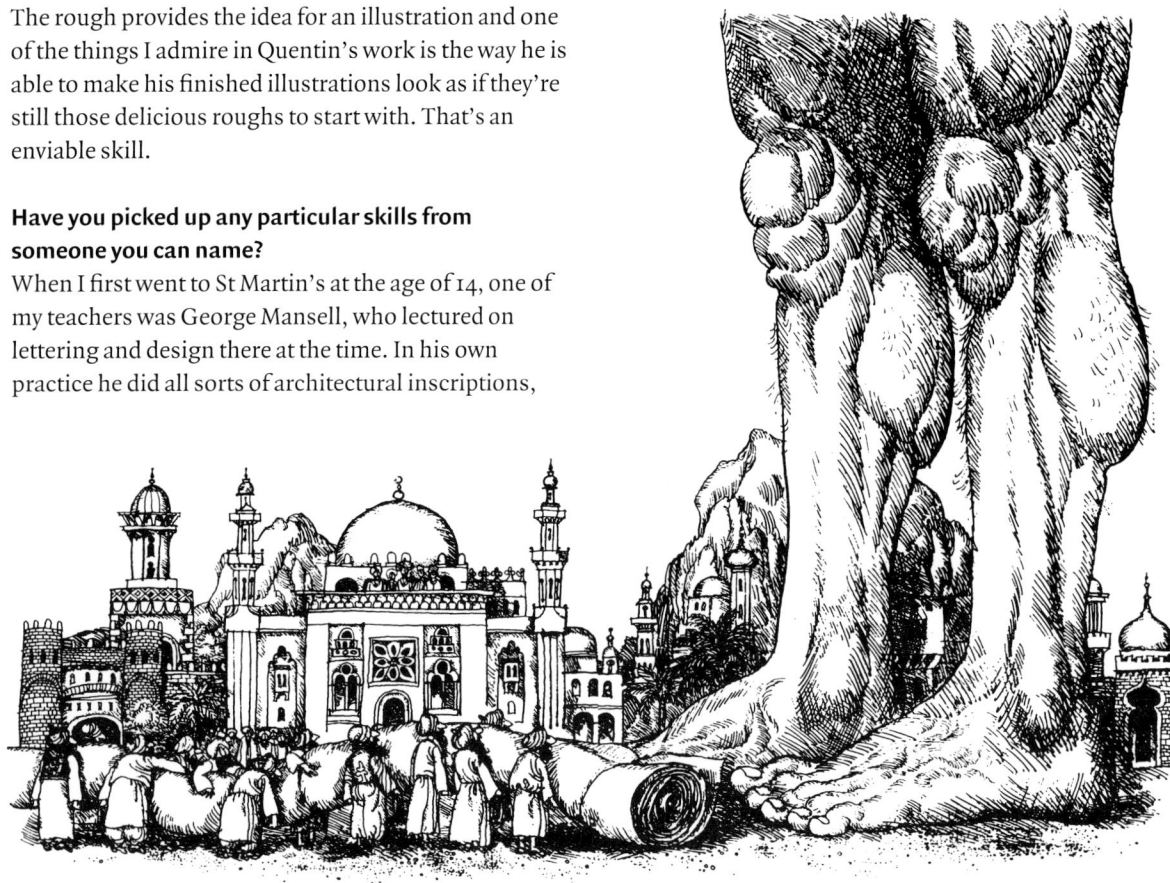

Fritz Wegner's

HEAVEN ON EARTH

ARIES
TAURUS
GEMINI
CANCER
LEO
VIRGO

LIBRA
SCORPIO
SAGITTARIUS
CAPRICORN
AQUARIUS
PISCES

Text by
Emma
Curzon

AN ASTROLOGICAL ENTERTAINMENT
with slides, wheels, and changing pictures

from Hamish Hamilton, for whom I worked over a number of years. I was teamed up with authors such as Dorothy L. Sayers, Raymond Chandler, Salinger, etc., whose first editions with my covers are now collectors' items. Among my favourites were two children's books: *The Hamish Hamilton Book of Princesses* and an accompanying one of *Princes*. They included some delightful classic Fairy Tales. *Mother Courage*, published by the Folio Society in 1965, is different in that I used a method for the illustrations that I hadn't attempted before. They were 'lift-ground' drawings: a cunning technique that makes them look like woodcuts. At that time, I was also given the chance to design my first set of postage stamps, and to everybody's surprise succeeded in winning the Christmas set design for 1969. Over the years I did a further eight sets of anniversary stamps, including a Valentine's stamp that earned me a trip to New York to talk to philatelists – a challenging experience!

Mother Courage, by Johann von Grimmelshausen, lift-ground drawings by Fritz Wegner, published by The Folio Society, London, 1965.

How do you see the role of the illustrator today?

Well, he or she can play quite an important role in the publishing world, perhaps less so in advertising now, but there are new opportunities in design, editorial work and animation. Where books are concerned, publishers need the odd best-seller to fund the books that don't do so well. If a book gets good reviews, or some other publicity, it will attract interest and sell more copies.

How do you get commissioned?

You may get teamed up with an author, or – better still – come up with a good project of your own. A publisher will pay you an advance, which then has to be paid back from your royalty earnings.

So, with *Fattypuffs & Thinifers*, for example?

Well, they didn't give illustrators royalties in those days. You were simply paid an outright fee. Although the book was produced in a number of other editions I never received any further payment. However, on this latest edition published by Jane Nissen, the cover for the book has been changed and I do receive a small royalty.

Your *Baron Munchausen* book has a really interesting layout. Did you have a say on how your illustrations would relate to the text?

Yes, I did. The drawings were an integral part of the design.

Commissioned by the Royal Mail, February, 1981.

Friendly Matches, written by
Allan Ahlberg, published
by Viking/Penguin,
London, 2001.

Right: The Hamish Hamilton
Book of Princes, stories
selected by Christopher
Sinclair-Stevenson,
published by Hamish
Hamilton, London, 1964.

The opening scene is a cucumber tree about to squash a couple; you captured the excitement rather than the horrific consequences of that...

Yes, I preferred to leave that to the imagination. The anticipation is more intriguing than the outcome. I really enjoyed doing these pictures. The *Munchausen*, of course, I remember from my own childhood days; likewise, *Grimm's Fairy Tales*, which I also illustrated years ago. More recently, another old time favourite I was asked to illustrate was *The Wicked Tricks of Till Owlyglass*, retold by Michael Rosen. Of course, as a boy, I knew the story as Till Eulenspiegel.

They could be quite gory scenes, couldn't they? Originally, children's books were often used to convey harsh moral warnings.

When I was doing my early children's books they were very careful not to do anything that would scare little children. But later on, after the publication of Sendak's *Where the Wild Things Are*, that seemed to break the mould and change attitudes. Before that, all the child psychologists were anxious not to frighten the little dears! Now, the more gory the drawings, the better they like them. Colin McNaughton has done some lovely ones in that genre.

What about your relationship with the authors?

Some authors are happy to leave the interpretation of the text to the illustrator, which is ideal. It's infinitely better because you're then given the freedom to do what you think is best. When authors have a very clear vision of what they want, they can tend to lean on you somewhat, which puts you in a more secondary role and can be a bit inhibiting.

You've done several books with Allan Ahlberg, haven't you?

Allan is a dear friend of mine, and he's always been extremely supportive to me. He likes what I do, and I appreciate that. And I admire what *he* does.

I've heard it described as a game of table tennis, where you both know where you're coming from and you both bounce off each other.

That's a good way of putting it. Allan is full of ideas; he's stimulating, and has a reputation for being a perfectionist. He had the ideal illustrator in his late wife, Janet, setting a style of enchanting humour that has been difficult to follow.

You have undertaken solo projects, haven't you?
Don't look now but it's Christmas again! **springs to mind.**

I used to submit drawings for the Christmas Show at Mel Calman's gallery, and when Patrick Hardy set up as a publisher with his own list he suggested I should do a series of drawings around the theme of Christmas and he would publish them. It was done in very quick time – 3 months – and I enjoyed it enormously. I was to do a follow-up one on the subject of love, but sadly Patrick died and regrettably the book never materialised.

You worked with your dear friend Emma Curzon on an incredible book, *Heaven on Earth*, an astrological entertainment with slides, wheels and changing pictures and all sorts...

Well, we did it between us. For some time, I had thought the subject rich in visual possibilities. Emma created all the words for the book – a very difficult task, especially as she had to distil a complicated subject and fit the text into limited spaces. The American co-edition did rather well, and it was very amusing to see it translated into Japanese – as well as French and Dutch.

Right: **Hullabaloo, an anthology edited by Barbara Willard, published by Hamish Hamilton Ltd, London, 1969.**

Don't look now but it's Christmas again!, **by Fritz Wegner, published by Patrick Hardy Books, London, 1983.**

Right: **The Wicked Tricks of Till Owlyglass, written by Michael Rosen, published by Walker Books, London, 1990.**

Are there any other artists you admire who have inspired you?

There are so many, I can hardly select a few. I love the early Renaissance, to start with; I love a great deal of early art of any kind – it fascinates me. I admire medieval manuscript art; the eighteenth- and nineteenth-century satirists like Daumier, Gilray, Rowlandson, Hogarth, Cruikshank, etc., and the more contemporary ones like George Grosz, Felix Topolski, Steinberg, and of course Ronald Searle and André François, who have been a great source of inspiration. In my teaching days, I regretted that students weren't more enriched in their imagination by all those exciting creations from the past.

So it's good to revert to the past?

Yes, I feel a certain amount of going back in time can be very healthy. Picasso admitted he learnt an awful lot from African art, and Monet found great inspiration from Japanese prints.

There are Picasso-like cats in the book you illustrated called *Carter is a Painter's Cat*. Would you call that a homage?

Well, yes. That was deliberate, of course. I mean, that was a skit.

You also drew a picture for the *Puffin Annual 2*, and you drew artefacts from your home.

I'm sorry you saw that! I must confess to letting my great collection of objects and books reveal themselves in my drawings. One of them is Christina, my lay figure; she's fully articulated and was made in France, around 1840. I remember bringing her to the house. She belonged to the family of a friend, who very kindly allowed me to buy her. I didn't have a car then, so I had to bring her home sitting beside me in a taxi. I carried her into the house like a new bride, which caused quite a stir in the neighbourhood. If you could see my studio you might well wonder where I find space to do my work. There isn't an inch of space on shelves, desks or floors – and yet I still search the markets and charity shops for ever more dubious treasures!

You popped in lots of Lear-like drawings in the *Puffin Annual*... I once drew a homage to Lear, and people said, 'Well, that's just a rip-off' and I said, 'Well actually, it's a homage to him.' Is there a line between those two, do you think?

What, a line between the homage and the rip-off?

Yes, ripping someone off or being lazy about your own work. Using someone else's style or idea?

Oh no, I think artists have used other artists' inspiration in their own work since time immemorial. That's a fairly common sort of thing to do and, freely admitted, one doesn't have to apologise for that.

So if I were to drop one of your Thinifers into a picture of mine in the future, you wouldn't mind?

Not at all. I would think it a compliment. In China, they repeated things over a thousand years on vases and paintings, and they even signed them with their characters of previous periods. That was not because they were slavishly copying, but because they were in awe of what was done before, and it was done by way of celebrating the past. We don't do that, but it was a known thing. You knew there was a convention there, so the work you see sometimes would have been done in the last century as well as in the twelfth century.

What do you like most about illustrating?

I love fanciful stories that give me lots of opportunities for invention and humour, because those are things I like to bring to my work. It's not the cartoony, belly-laugh type of humour, but something perhaps a little more subtle. I don't like crude jokes, and I'm not a great funny-story-teller.

I think your books tell them all, don't they?

I suppose I do see the funny side of life.

Do you put that down to anything in particular?

What would I put it down to? I don't know where it comes from. It's the way one is; it's part of one's make-up. I remember when I was a child, I used to clown in the classroom by doing cartoons, but the one time I got into really serious trouble over my silly drawings was when Hitler invaded Austria during the Anschluss. I thought it would be a bit of a laugh to picture him with the little moustache he had – you know he was an easy one to caricature. It created an outrage, of course, and the teacher in the class was a dedicated Nazi; he even came in uniform on one occasion with his swastikas all over him. My cartoon of Hitler – rather innocent, you may think – was shown to him. I got a belting for it and was thrown out of class. Later on, of course, I was thrown out of the school altogether, so that was it. So my humour didn't always pay off. It misfired on that occasion.

But you weren't thrown out of the school for your cartooning?

Not for that, but because I was Jewish. And that's something else I didn't really fully comprehend because I never thought about it. I was brought up in a very liberal-minded household, where religion didn't feature. Until the Nazi days, I didn't think I was any different from anyone else. I was never treated differently. It just suddenly came out of the blue and it was a horrible shock to me to be discriminated against and punished for it. Anyway, as you can see, I survived over all those years, and here I am, talking to you at the Chelsea Arts Club. Life can dish up a few things along the way that one has to learn to cope with.

I'd like to thank Fritz for his time and company. A real gentleman, generous, kind and hugely inspirational.

Baron Munchausen's Marvellous Travels & Adventures, by R. E. Raspe & others, adapted and introduced by Janet Barber, published by The Bodley Head, London, 1967.

Facing page: Puffin Annual, **Number one,** edited by Treld Bicknell, Frank Waters & Kaye Webb, published by Puffin Books a division of Penguin Books Ltd, London, 1974.

Jacob Two Two Meets the Hooded Fang written by Mordecai Richler, a Borzoi book published by Alfred A. Knopf, Inc., New York, 1975.

Puffin Annual

A proud moment P

I think so

Are we the first?

Keep the ranks men

Move over

The Faithless Lollybird

The Cat

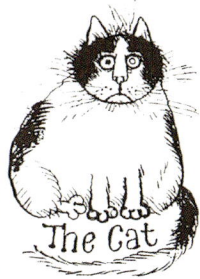

The Boy, the Dog and the Spaceship

Professor Branestawm Goes Cuckoo

La Corona and the Tin Frog

10 Characters in Search of an Author

The Upside Down Mice

How to make a Puffin Kite

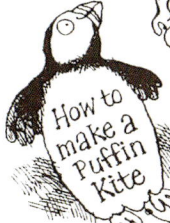

That Awful Boy

Captain Pugwash on TV

Here Be Dragons

My Mother's Frilly Parasol

HOW Birds Fly

Putting a Ship in a Bottle

Poems Puzzles Cartoons Magic Smilers & Scowlers

Authors and Places

The Strange Affair of the Wattle-U-EAT

PICTURE Stories in COLOUR

Collecting Castles

Amazing Achievements

Looking at Paintings

of Days Gone By

The children's books of Květa Pacovská

Wendy Coates-Smith

Květa Pacovská was born in Prague in 1928, and graduated from the Academy of Applied Arts, Prague, in 1952. Her work has been exhibited in many countries and her books translated into German, Japanese, French, Italian, Portuguese, Dutch and Chinese. Among her numerous honours have been the Golden Apple at the BIB in Bratislava 1983, the Grand Prix of the Premi Catalonia in Barcelona 1988, the German Children's Literature Award 1991, the Hans Christian Andersen 1992 and the Sankei Children's Books Culture Award/Fuji Television Award for the best children's book of the year 2000.

Květa Pacovská is essentially an artist with her roots in European Modernism. She studied fine art and is responsive to the concerns of other sculptors and painters. In this respect the nature of her materials, metal, canvas, paint and paper, is of primary importance to her. But perhaps more than these essentials and her creative use of them is her use of colour, light and space. Her inspiration has been derived from cultural sources as diverse as music and dance, and the powerful ideas which emanated from artists associated with the Dada movement and the Bauhaus. Though she learned about books and how to make them, the Czech tradition of book illustration has never been reflected in her work. Her illustrations have been published in the special editions of *Graphis*[1] magazine devoted to children's book illustration. Sufficiently well established and esteemed to appear in surveys of Czech illustration, her affiliations are entirely personal.

The complex web of cultural influence defies categorisation, and so complete is her transformation of the material from which she has derived nourishment that any attempt to trace these threads to their source, as a means of explaining her 'phenomenon', is futile. She will say that she admires the work of Ben Nicholson or Anthony Caro, and something of that admiration may inform her sculpture, nevertheless her total concept of art, embracing sound and colour, means that all the individual elements combine and recombine in her exhibitions causing our perceptions of her identity to undergo shifts of emphasis. In a space without any

natural light, she will choreograph the lighting so that she controls the shadows created by the work on the wall. Her principal material above all is paper. Her artist's books may be large and weighty as with *Paper Paradise*[2] and *Scrap*[3] but they celebrate in a tender and sensuous manner the way in which paper and its material properties, printed and unprinted, torn and cut, offer a responsive surface for marks and also the effects of colour and light.

1. Graphis Children's Books, Amstutz and Herdeg, Zurich, 1967.
2. *Paper Paradise*, Homage to Kurt Schwitters, an artist's book of pages printed by lithography and cut to reveal other layers, Pravis, Verlag, Osnabruck, 1991.
3. *Scrap*, an artist's book which pays tribute to the cast off, the off cut and the scrap, Edition Aulos, Prague, 1997.

A page from *Paper Paradise* the homage to Kurt Schwitters taken from *The Art of Květa Pacovská*.

Cat from *The Art of Kvĕta Pacovská*.

development of each individual child, who may return again and again to her books, discovering quite different things each time.

This variable and supple interpretation of her work, and its reinterpretation by the child over time varies according to the intention of the book. In the case of *The Little Flower King*,[4] this is a traditional text interpreted in a creative visuality which is rich and tender and voluptuous. Her marks are perhaps the most deliberate and quantifiable things she does. What makes the experience magic for the child is the invitation to explore the colour and spatial opportunities offered, especially through the books such as *Alphabet*,[5] which have no text. Pacovská appreciates that her books will find a different response in each child, and the process of communication is renewed through these differences. There is a sense in which her creative ideas progress and develop within her own creative journey, and it may be seen that her earlier works for children are more obviously based on traditional patterns, but these do not prevent the child responding to her recent work, notably *Paper City*,[6] a book published in Japan for the Japanese market. All her books contain an element of 'interactivity' within themselves, but her books are equally accessible to the same child through an interactivity of the heart.

Her familiar companions are the Clown, the Sun and Moon, and creatures such as the Cat and the Lion, but her fascination also lies in her capacity to surprise, and so Snails and Rhinoceros, as well as the Frog and the Hippotumus attend her tender celebrations.

An important quest for Pacovská has been to find ways in which her concepts of art may inform her children's books. She believes that the child 'takes everything in' and must therefore be given the finest materials and ideas. These are not be found in expensive toys or luxurious objects but objects of a natural kind such as stones or pieces of fabric. Before she could read, she would sit alone in a room, in the presence of books, experiencing them as objects – their colour, texture and smell. It has taken her many years to find ways in which her books may be accessible to children beyond the public arena of her exhibitions and installations, and to excite the mind of the child through the colour and texture of her books. She associates letters and colours with sounds, and in sitting with children while they explore her books, engages them in the process of articulating the sounds associated with the colours and shapes.

Sound is an important element in her choice of colour and Pacovská says of her reaction to colour:[7]

Colour. White and black are not included in the colour spectrum but for me they are colours and mean maximum contrast. And maximum contrast is the maximum beauty. I am striving for maximum contrast. Red and green. The placing of colours one over the other. It depends on the relation, proportion, rhythm, size, amount and how we place colours together. It is like music. Each individual tone is beautiful by itself and in certain groupings we can create new dimensions, harmony, disharmony, symphonies, operas and books for children.

Pacovská is an artist whose passion has been expressed in innumerable ways. But, for the purposes of this introduction, the emphasis must be on her contribution to the world of children's books. Radical in the context of English children's books, where the narrative tradition is so powerfully developed and the impetus to children's publishing is primarily based on the impulse to tell a story, Pacovská's commitment is to a more ethereal approach. Her books, which exert a powerful spell on the reader, do so because she is concerned with experiences which are not linked to the visualisation of a text – though she is quite capable of doing this – but to a more total experience of the book as a means to link the spirit to the adventure of turning the page.

But this is not the turning of a page to discover what happens next, but to engage in an open-ended journey through the imagination. Her books are a means for travel through the child's own imagination. And for this reason mean not only quite different things from one child to another, but also within the personal

4. *The Little Flower King*, a Michael Neugebauer Book, Verlag Neugebauer Press, Salzburg, 1991.

5. *Alphabet*, Ravensburger Buchverlag, Germany, 1996.

6. *Paper City*, Editor Yasushi Oka, Shogakukan Inc. 3–1 Hitotsubashi 2-chrome, Chiyoda-ku, Tokyo, 101–8001 Japan, 2001.

7. *The Art of Kvĕta Pacovská*, Dr Barbara Scharioth, Michael Neugebauer Verlag AG, Gossau-Zürich/Frankfurt/ Salzburg, 1993.

It is possible for her ideas to be applied to artefacts of diverse size and material because her sense of scale may be adapted to apply to small paper or card maquettes or to sheets of metal several feet high. So her exhibitions which contain a table of small paper 'cities' may also contain sculptures the height of a man.

Two quite different artists are called to my mind when looking at her work. The first, a composer, is Stravinsky; the second an American sculptor, Louise Nevelson. In their different ways she acknowledges their power and the energy she finds inspirational. Stravinsky represents the potential of music to generate imagery and to provide the theatrical elements she needs to feed on, and the context in which her work may exist. Until her health prevented it, she studied ballet, and saw a career as a dancer might be possible – as well as that of an artist. *Midnight Play*[8] perfectly illustrates her appreciation of the stage as a literal and metaphoric place for her characters to congregate, and realise their dreams in a magical way.

This is in part a split book, which allows the child to create their own character, and give it a special name. The story is a simple structure in which the Moon beams down and wakes the clown. In his turn the Clown invites the Moon to attend a performance in the theatre. The child then uses the multitude of split page characters to create a story to their liking, and employ the wonderful crazy combinations of names and personalities. All the while, the Moon may travel through the pages on a piece of string, and when not in use, be lodged in a special place on the board cover of the book.

The association with Nevelson was prompted for me by her love of monochromatic effects, for instance the impact of shadows on the pages of a book when parts of the proceeding page have been cut away.

MIDNIGHTPLAY

KVĚTA PACOVSKÁ

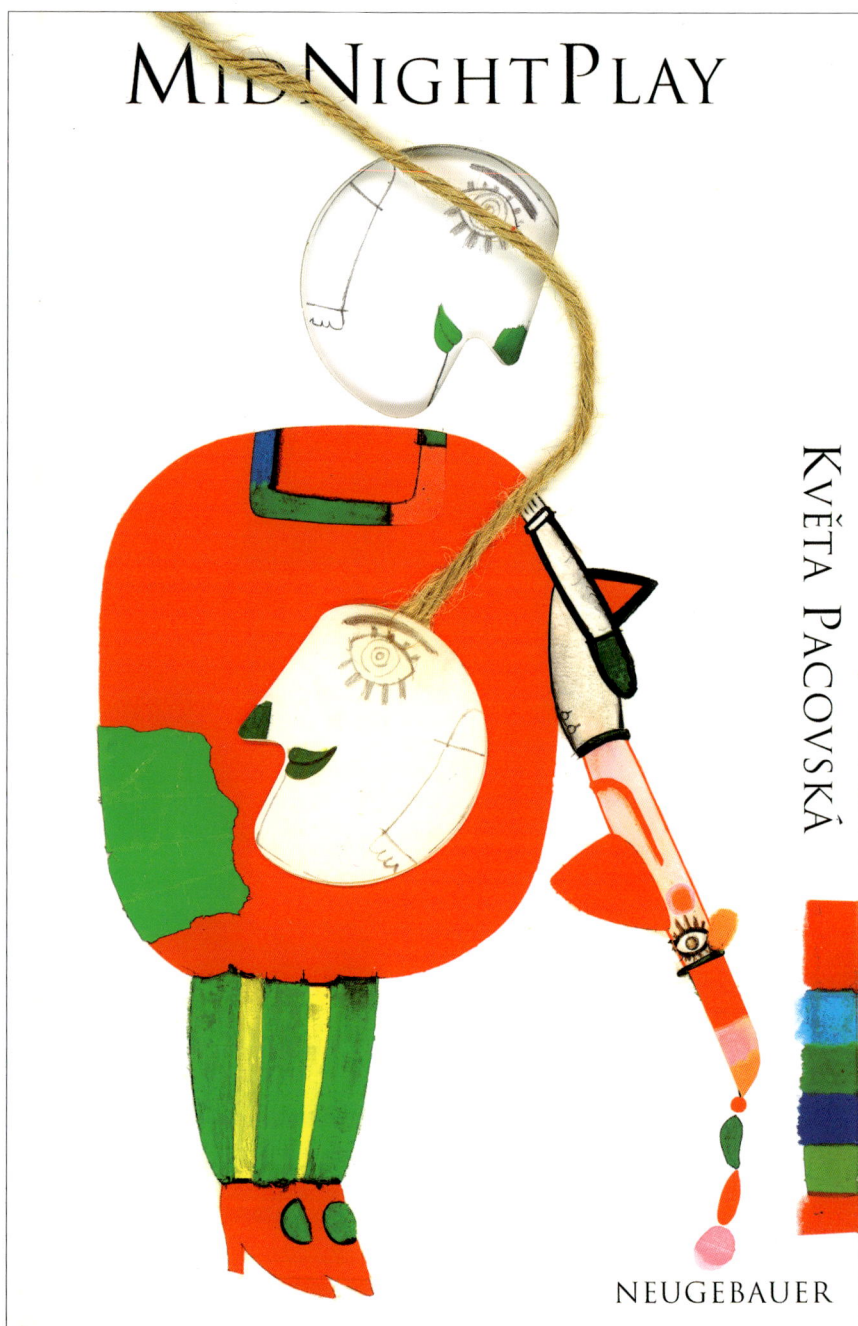

MIDNIGHTPLAY

KVĚTA PACOVSKÁ

NEUGEBAUER

Pacovská was profoundly affected by the experience of sitting in her father's library and relating to the books as objects. Row upon row of book spines, each catching the light in a different way and producing a modulated sculptural effect might well have been her first encounter with simple three-dimensional forms and the way in which these change depending on the direction and intensity of the light.

We discussed the sculpture of Nevelson, and we discovered something of which she was unaware, namely that Nevelson had herself been inspired by the Merzbau work of Kurt Schwitters.

Nevelson is supposed to have described Schwitters as her 'spiritual grandfather' and the possibilities of the Hanover Merzbau, developed by Schwitters, were not lost on Nevelson. These links, though not particularly unusual in themselves, simply underline the wide frame of creative reference on which Pacovská has drawn. Pacovská, as with all powerful creators working across several disciplines – printmaking, illustration,

Cover for Midnight Play shows the resting place of the moon before the action begins.
Title page (*left*)**, the curtains go up.**

8. *Midnight Play*, Picture Book Studio, Neugebauer Press International, Salzburg, London, 1992.

sculpture and painting – transforms and unifies exactly those particles which combined together produce fresh meanings, or clarify partly developed ones.

One of the main consequences of these explorations are the books for children. And it is these which have demonstrated best how Pacovská has brought art into the world of the child. The experience of holding and examining her children's books is a spiritual one, and a joyful one too.

In conversation with Květa Pacovská
Wednesday 6th December 2000

Inside pages for *Midnight Play*. *Below:* **split pages showing a figure which my be made by the reader.** *Right:* **a playful game in which names can change, while the moon looks on.**

What were your childhood experiences of books?
It is difficult to say because it was not with a specific book – it was before I could read. But I experienced the atmosphere of books. I would often sit alone in my father's library which was at home. There were a lot of books bound in leather, on science and natural history, and encyclopaedias. I was alone and free to do what I wanted. The books were something between objects which I could touch and feel, and something through which I could travel in my mind. This was my first experience of books and a very deep one for me because the atmosphere of the books was so very very interesting.

What other elements of play did you have in childhood, toys for instance, or games?
There was nothing in particular, beside a game which involved tiny balls. These small balls were in natural colours such as Puzzola, Coin Blue and Dirty Yellow and were made from a cheap material, mostly ceramic. You had to get them in a small hole, then you were the winner and took all the balls yourself. Many years later I used this game in some of my 'Works'.

I liked simple things like stones, pieces of fabric or objects which could form other associations – and I loved old objects like buttons or badges. The experiences you have as a child are very important because you take it in and it can last forever. That is why it is necessary to give beautiful experiences because the influence is going to go on. We take it all inside.

Were there other kinds of art forms that had an impact on your imagination, like music?
I enjoyed music very much. I loved old music. Especially Gregorian chant because it has for me some connection with colours. My father sang in the opera – there is a photograph of him in *The Art of Květa Pacovská* as he appeared as the moor in Othello in 1908.

When did your gift for art begin to show itself?
I do not like to divide up this – I always made art. It has been so continuous that I cannot remember a time when I didn't make art. I am my art, my art is me!

But many children start by drawing, and making art – and then they don't continue.

Yes, you are right. The child makes art directly from the emotional feeling that they get from working on paper and then they go to school and the teacher says 'This is nice!' and 'This is not nice!' and 'This shouldn't be done in this way!' and they lose the natural way of working which is directly connected to their imagination. I went to the common school and forgot all about myself and my ideas, but my education was interrupted by the war. The Germans came when I was eleven and I lost so many years that afterwards I decided to go directly to Art School. The war changed my life completely. The library was ruined and my father was sent to the camps. I never saw him again.

At the Academy of the Applied Arts they teach you how to make books and how to illustrate books. I never studied illustration, I studied painting at the Academy of Applied Arts with professor Emil Filla, a great personality, but I have done pictures for some very beautiful texts for books. Now I have my own ideas and have developed a more global approach to the book where I am concerned with all the aspects and how they combine – the text, the images, the letter forms, the page size, the paper – its texture, colour and smell. Everything. All the time I wanted to get the qualities I liked in my painting into my books. Although the last ten years have allowed me to push my ideas further.

In each book I have tried to to keep some level of art, and I didn't want to describe what is beautifully explained by the text. I was trying to create a third level – not at this time for touch, but aspects for the eyes. I was seeking to be more cosmopolitan, more universal. My feeling for art is not just for Czechoslovakian influences, but I am for example very close to Prague as a city. I love all cities and maybe Prague is a beautiful city, but it's my city. I was born here so I have connection with the culture. For me for example there are important ideas in Gothic art and sculpture as well. But then its not just Prague, there are connections with other cities. Cities concentrate art together and allow the connections between art – of good and bad in art. You find the galleries and the art which is inspiring and when I go in it is the same feeling that I had in my father's library as a very small child.

In particular you illustrated *Rootabaga Stories* by Carl Sandburg 1965, and later *The Lord of the Flies* by William Golding in 1968, besides editions of poetry and fairy stories. How did the change in 1990 come about?

I won my first award for *The Rootabaga Stories*. The

Above and left: **two spreads from *One Five Many*.**

Facing page: **cover and two spreads from *The Little Flower King*.**

PICTURE BOOK STUDIO
ISBN 0-88708-221-1

KVĚTA PACOVSKÁ THE LITTLE FLOWER KING

THE LITTLE
FLOWER KING
BY KVĚTA PACOVSKÁ

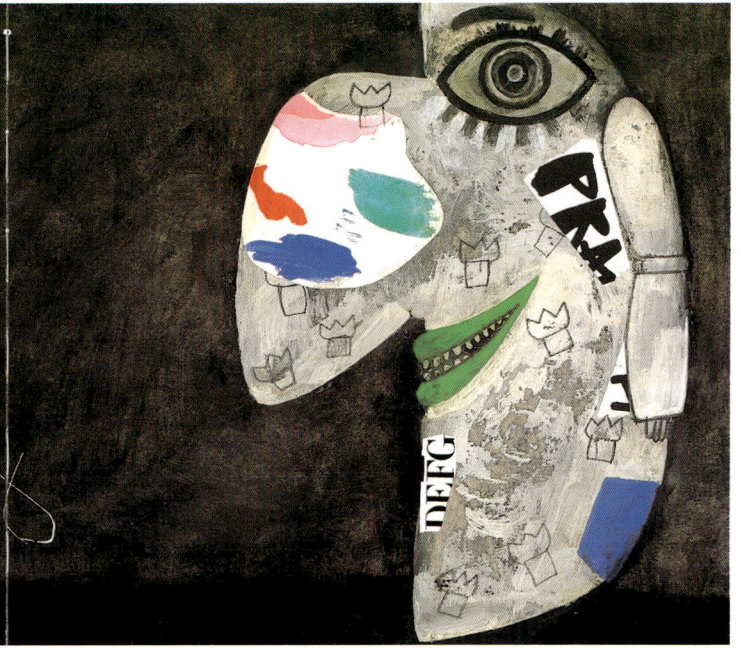

O weh ! jammert die Schnecke, die mit ihrem
Haus traurig durch die Welt wandert. O weh !
Oh ! weint sie laut, als sie den Frosch sieht.
Wer gibt mir ein bißchen Rot ? Ach, ach, ach je !
Ach je ! Ach, ach, ach ! Wer gibt mir nur ein
bißchen Gelb ? Hu, hu, hu ! Hu, hu, hu, hu, hu !
Ach, hätte ich doch nur ein bißchen Grün !
Hie, hie, hie, hie, hie, hie ! Schau doch, schau,
hier wünsche ich mir ein bißchen Blau !
Oh, oh, oh, oh, oh ! Oh ! Oh ! Warum gibt mir
niemand ein bißchen Orange ?

Huu-huu !

Huu-huu !

Huuhuuhuuu !

Huuhuuhuuu !

Hu, huu !

O weh !

O weh !

O weh !

O weh !

Hör doch auf ! sagt der Frosch.

Geh weg,
dummer   Frosch !
grau !
grau, nur grau ?
hellgrau   weißgrau
dunkelgrau
schwarzgrau
ganz schwarz

Hie, hie, hie, hie, hie…
Huu-huu, hu, huu, huuhuuhuuu !
Oh, oh, oh, oh !

Oh, oh, oh, oh !
Hu, hu, hu ! Hu, hu, hu, hu !
Hu! Hu! Hu! Hu!
Hu, hu, hu! Hu, hu, hu !

97
1,2,3,4,5,6,7
JZλX

Hör doch auf ! sagt der Frosch wieder.

stories were written when Carl Sandburg had two small
daughters, and you know often the text for children's
books is not as good as it should be. But these stories
I enjoyed very much and the text has great quality.
I illustrated *Lord of the Flies* because I loved the text.
Literature is very important to me and I would love to do
Alice in Wonderland by Lewis Carroll. All my life I wanted
to do that book! Surprisingly I also love the edition with
the Tenniell illustrations. Sometimes I want to put the
illustrations away because they do not feed my
imagination. But *Alice in Wonderland* can be read by
someone of any age and enjoyed because it is so
powerful.

All this time I had been experimenting to make
books which would bring my ideas about art into my
books. This began somewhere in the sixties. I had been
working on these ideas for many years, and trying to
get them published. Then suddenly a German
publisher wanted them. He had seen an exhibition of
my paintings and sculptures and there are a lot of
paper objects, books which explored space. He wanted
to publish my ideas which was very nice because
I didn't have to ask. It was a miracle! Objects and
sculptures made of paper are part of my exhibitions.
It has taken from the late sixties until the nineteen
nineties to get the ideas into print.

Two spreads from *Rund und Eckig*.

Ich bin ein Kater,

ein Quadrat,

ein Vogelreiter.

Ich bin ein Klang in einer Sonate.

9. *One Five Many*, published by Ravensburger Buchverlag Otto Maier GmbH, Germany, 1996.

10. *Grun Rot Alle*, published by Ravensburger Buchverlag Otto Maier GmbH, Germany, 1992.

Overleaf
Verso: **three spreads from *Alphabet*.**
Recto: **cover and two spreads from *Corne Rouge*.**

Tell me about the books, which was the first?

One Five Many.[9] It was published in German, French and English in 1990. The clown and the hippopotamus take us through the numbers One to Ten. The child looks at a picture and can also look through them to what is behind. You can put your finger in the hole – that is page 1. You can close your eyes and pass your finger over the embossed shapes. The rhythm of each double spread is important, it shows us the form of the numeral and the quantity. So it is an experience that is shared in horizontal and vertical position with the clown and the hippopotamus. I was thinking that this might be the first one and the last and nobody will want to buy the book, but it sold immediately out and won a big prize.

The second one, published in 1992 was about colour, *Grun Rot Alle*,[10] or in France *Couleur Couleurs*. I chose a snail because its form allowed me to use the device of the colour wheel. I always pick animals I like. It may be because they are big or I need their form to play with. Two animals, a snail and a frog, tell the story. They are the poorest of the poor. It is very dark and they have nothing, only their dreams about colour. The pages show their lamentation and also that the rain is not always without colour. The wheel which is the snail house shows the possibilities of white, clear grey and black. The colour wheel is a classical tool in the history of art – but here it is a device so that the snail can colour his house. The frog and the snail are transformed by

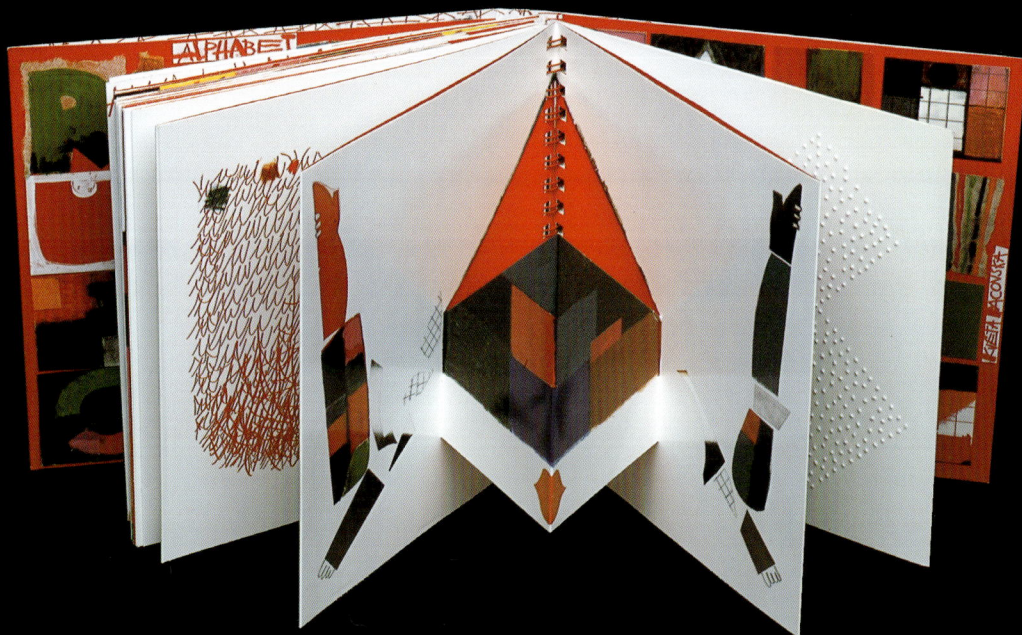

« Soyons amis », dit-il aussi

samedi,

Rhino-pois

et de

tâtons.

Lundi,

Mercredi

tout rouge

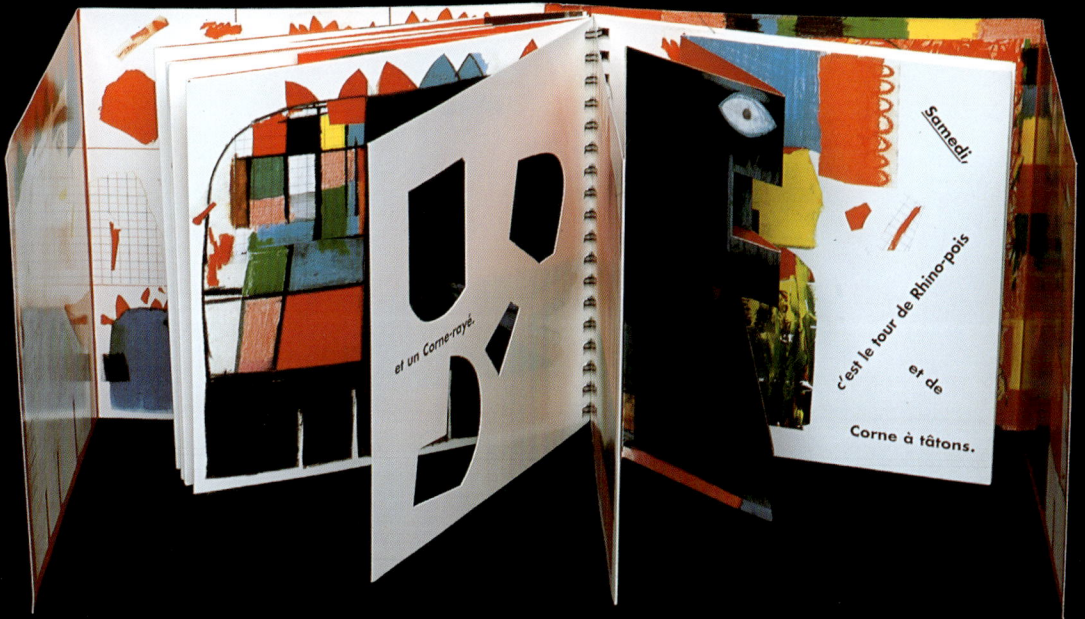

et un Corne-rayé.

samedi,

c'est le tour de Rhino-pois

et de

Corne à tâtons.

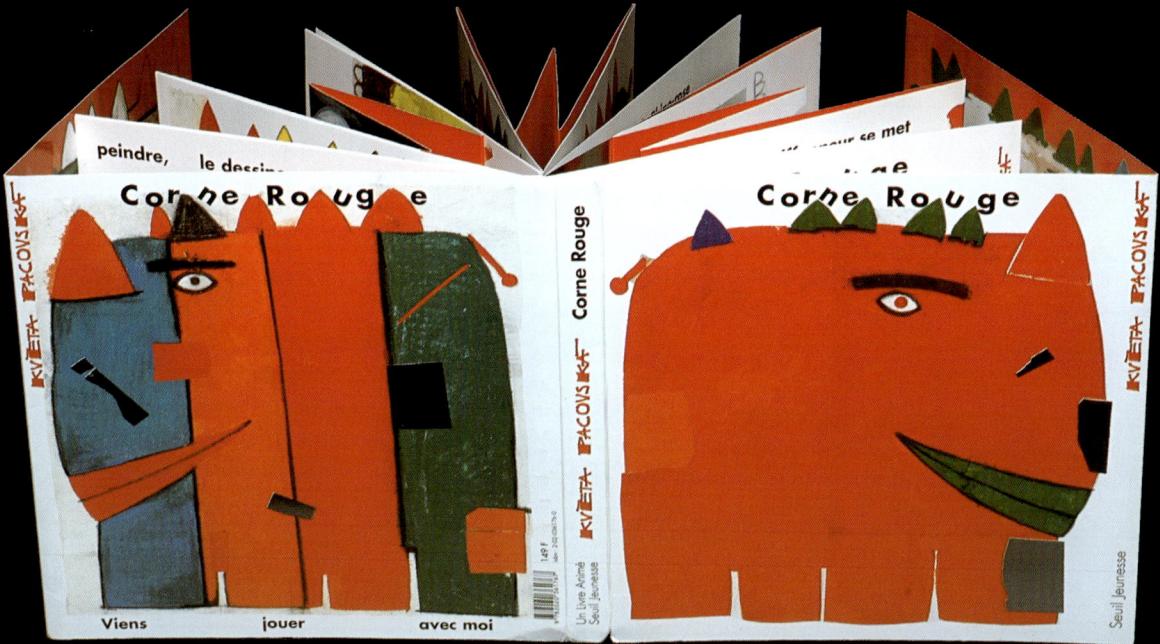

peindre,   le dessin

Corne Rouge

Corne Rouge

Corne Rouge

KVĚTA PACOVŠ

Viens   jouer   avec moi

Un livre Animé
Seuil Jeunesse

Seuil Jeunesse

something of the quality of ballet, of making art through your own body... and if you don't see the moon in the sky it is because he is sitting in the theatre.

Double spread from *Paper City*.

their discovery of colour and can go into the countryside of crayons. If somebody knows further beautiful colours they should put them in the book.

***The Little Flower King* and *Midnight Play* were also published in 1992. *Midnight Play* is also a book about transformation, but through a narrative process which can be repeated over and over again, allowing the child to control or interpret the story as they want.**

The Little Flower King was translated into eighteen/nineteen languages and became an 'evergreen'. It is not only an interactive book with the cut square in the middle of the page, but it is also a 'Love Story'.

I loved working on *Midnight Play*, it is an important book for me because it takes place in a theatre, and because of the possibilities offered for endless variation. You are free to create your own character. There is also

Then in 1994 I did a book about shapes, called *Rund und Eckig*.[11] It's an adventure and I made it like a paper sculpture. The shapes such as the cube, the circle, the triangle and the line which describes the shape are demonstrated through the meeting with a series of characters and things. These do not fit into any system but follow the things I want to show. The circle is both a button and a wheel. The cube is represented as the body of a cat or the muzzle of a lion. The triangle is a clown's face or a series of feathers on a bird's body. So the interpretation of the forms is broad and encourages the child's imagination and to look carefully at the world around, even the most ordinary things or maybe especially the most ordinary things.

11. *Rund und Eckig*, published by Ravensburger Buchverlag Otto Maier GmbH, Germany, 1994.

12. *Alphabet*, published by Ravensburger Buchverlag, Germany, 1996.

You can stand the book up, it is important that the books can stand. You can look into the space and see the pictures behind, and the reflections which the foil gives and these in turn give reflections and shadows. The spaces which appear when the book is stood up allow the child to 'walk through' the space. I have done this with many children over the years, pleased how they react to these sensations.

When you worked on *Alphabet* these ideas could progress further without the limitations of text, your books are translated into too many languages for text to work in each of these languages.

Yes, *Alphabet*[12] was published in 1996. I wrote a piece about *Alphabet* called The Architecture of Pleasure. You can close your eyes and explore the spaces with your finger tips and discover the sensations offered there.

Pages which are punctured with small holes or cuts or folds which go to make the letter forms bring to life another kind of experience of books. My picture books for children make no compromises. They have an aesthetic and artistic message as strong as any in fine art. It is a book to look at in the usual way, at each double spread – whatever you want. You can also deconstruct the book and take each letter out. I did this once for one of my exhibitions.

So I have shown that it is possible to do other things. We can look at each letter, touch each letter, listen to each letter – each letter has its own sound, its own form, its own duration, its own colour. If you 'say' it in English, 'AAAA', aloud, then you can listen to the sound and the sound has a colour.

I have tried this with children in France and Japan and the sounds are quite different. So the book is interactive.

That was my idea for another interactive book, *Corne Rouge*[13] which came out in 1999. This covers the days of the week, and on every day the child makes a paper friend, from Sunday to Saturday. You can make the things in the book, or just look at it on the table. The book is based on a red rhino – another big animal. The red rhino is celebrated in colours and made gorgeous for children.

I was interested to hear what you had to say about your appreciation of cities, and if this played a part in the development of your latest book *Paper City*?
It came about because I have been making paper cities all my life, and I love to create paper cities for a space somewhere. Sometimes I design it to be large enough for a small person to walk through, for an exhibition or for a museum and in other circumstances my paper city will stay on a table. I want to show this aspect of my work because arranging paper cities is also part of my art. I do it because it gives me enormous pleasure and it makes no difference what scale I work with.

These ideas can exist in a book where the cut pages allow selected parts of the image to show through, and where the shadows cast by the cuts are part of the experience. In a room the pictures hang quietly on the walls and are glimpsed through the labyrinths. You can sit in this space and it is an elegant space for meditation.

I cannot imagine you finding the same satisfaction in bricks and mortar, since once it is made it cannot be reconfigured in the same way that your paper sculptures can, and have the same sort of multiple interpretations?
When I think about a city I can make it, then move it. It would be wonderful if someone would make a library with an exhibition space where I could make my paper cities. That would be beautiful.

When the Japanese invited me to make the book, I wanted to call it *Paper Talks*. But we agreed to change it to *Paper City* and that was also fine and in tune with my direction. It was a very lovely and intensive collaboration.

Sometimes I am asked to explain my art, but I don't want to explain it because my explanation will cut off the personal response. It may be like music which at first you don't understand, but after listening many times you understand more and more and you find your own way to that over time. You have to reach out and trust to your own response.

She described her ideas about colour to Giovanna Pastega in an interview for the exhibition of her work at the Museo Biblioteca Archivio Bassano del Grappa.

...There are for me two fundamental considerations in illustrations for children: and these are light and contrast. As far as beauty is concerned , all colours are equal, only that they have different souls. And hence, the really important thing, when you are painting, is how to put them together, how to make their souls live happily together, to create in their facing and confronting each other in their basic essence, strong feeling in who sees them.

Look, colours are a fundamental thing in whatever communication, for the simple reason that they are emotional 'vectors'. Being in a red room or a blue room is not the same thing: what thy lead you to feel is completely different. And the same thing holds true for a secret room full of colours and emotions for whoever discovers it.

Light, like colour, has a strong emotional effect, extraordinary in its power to change one's perception of things, their form, their colours and thus what one feels about and with them. Not only in sculpture is light particularly emotively important for the way it arrives, how it strikes the sculpture and the shadows it creates on the walls. It changes the perception of the work of art and therefore the feeling it arouses. This is why the work of art is not an isolated entity but always has to do with its environment and who is looking at it.

13. *Corne Rouge*, published by Ravensburger Buchverlag, Germany, 1999.

Page from *Paper City*.

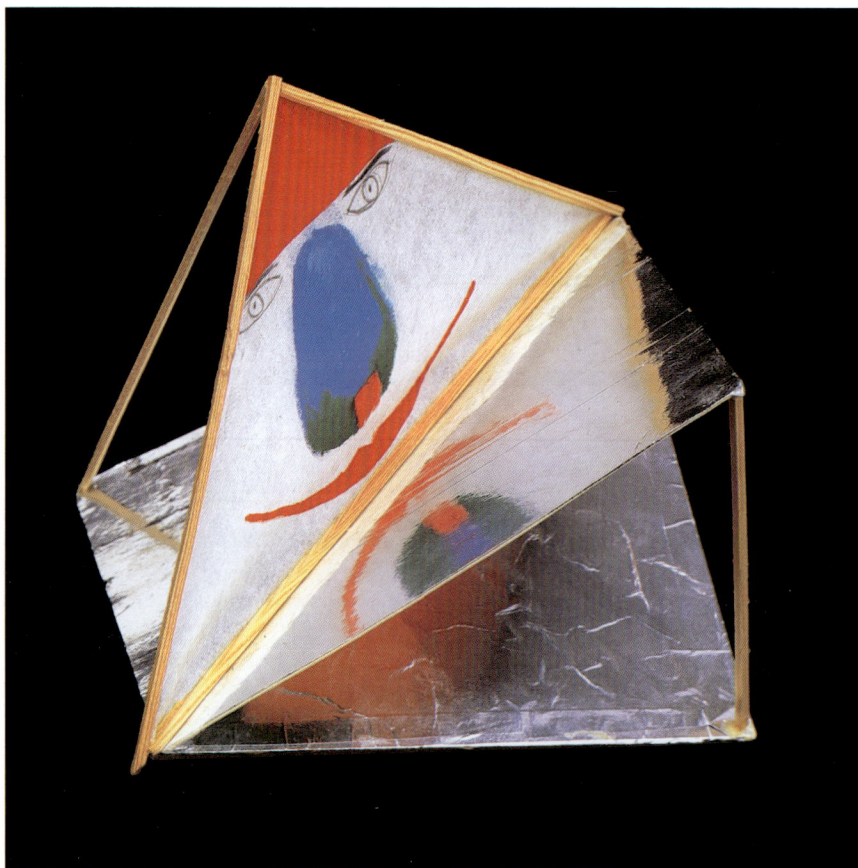